To David

Best of Luck

Jes R. Herrera

4/26/92

MEMORIES

OF MY

LIFE

Jess
Robert
Herrera

MEMORIES OF MY LIFE

Published by Jess R. Herrera.

Printed and bound in the United States of America.

Library of Congress Catalog Card Number: 91-92483

ISBN 1-881156-00-1

Photograph of Helms Powerhouse courtesy of Pacific Gas & Electric Company.

JESS ROBERT HERRERA
1924 -

MY JOURNEY

Life's journey has taken me down nature's paths. Some paths have led into wooded spires of dense forest lands, some to the very top of rocky mountain peaks, some to the edge of vast arid deserts and great rolling plains, some to the muddy banks of rushing rivers and on to the very brink of the ocean's surging tidal waves, some to the quiet peace of tiny hamlets, and some to the din and bustle of the world's largest cities.

But no matter what path, the human spirit has soared within me, the mind has been ever searching, and the heart has sought compassion for fellow man and yearned for love of family and the Lord.

But that is in the past, and the present days bring new beginnings. What the future holds only He knows. So with trust in the Lord and until the end, our imperfect self strives for life's fulfillment. Our hope is to continue to stay on the path and not to stray, and thus to finish the journey in an honorable way.

JRH

CONTENTS

DEDICATION

THIS BOOK IS DEDICATED TO MY WIFE ALICIA,
AND TO MY CHILDREN AND GRANDCHILDREN.

MAY GOD ALWAYS KEEP THEM UNDER
HIS PROTECTION.

ACKNOWLEDGMENTS

This section is not an attempt on my part to thank those many individuals who have helped me throughout my life. That would be an impossible task because how can anyone adequately thank their parents, sisters, and brother, and immediate family, and relatives, and countless involved friends for their love, guidance, sacrifices, understanding, and helping hand? Even so, I am grateful for their support, and everyone of them has my appreciation.

These acknowledgments are mainly directed towards the writing of this book.

I owe a general acknowledgment and thanks to my dear wife, Alicia, for her encouragement and sharing of my enthusiasm for this difficult and unique book writing effort. She also proofread the original drafts of each chapter and offered many helpful comments.

All my children also were instrumental in my perseverance on this project because of their interest.

Additionally, Gloria my daughter gave me a paperback book by Frank P. Thomas on "How To Write the Story of Your Life". This book and many others I referred to from the Public Library served as useful references.

Albert, my son, helped immensely in getting the book formatted and ready for reproduction into final book form. I thank him for his efforts and time.

Richard, my son, his wife Suzi, and Paul Love, a

6

friend, helped in trying to find a suitable print shop.

I obtained some of my ancestral information from previous records search work done by Jose Flores, my cousin. My thanks also go to him for sharing his research.

Finally, Carol at Moody Graphics, San Francisco, helped me with the cover design.

INTRODUCTION

The thought of writing about my past life had never entered my mind. However, just before retiring from work at age 65, I naturally looked back on my past life and tried to reflect on what had happened all the previous years. What had I done with my life? What had been the turning points with my family and in my career? What had I accomplished to date, and how had I gotten to this point in my life?

In a way, I had some of the answers fresh in my mind because in recent years, I had shared some of my past experiences with student ethnic minorities. I had been trying to encourage these youngsters to work hard and get a good education to achieve their potential, in spite of possible economic hardships and an unsupporting social environment. I had tried to be an example and a role model for them. They listened because they realized, that in my background, I had previously faced some of the same obstacles they were now facing.

Furthermore, in three or four instances, my career had been profiled in publications as human interest stories because of being an Hispanic in a high Corporate position. I was a rare subject. Each of these stories had included a summary background of my past life. As a result, these published articles elicited much interest among readers.

So upon reflection, I decided that if perfect strangers found my past interesting, then certainly my own family would also want to know more details about me than they already knew. Also, in the future, my descendants could use this record to find out something about their ancestors. So after retirement, I decided to write this book; basically to provide information for my children, my grandchildren, and my great grandchildren. It is my hope that by reading this book it will serve as an inspiration to them as they journey through life.

As the title implies, the book is a gathering of certain selected memories from different periods in my life. It is not an encyclopedic collection of everything that has transpired during my lifetime. It covers only highlights, special events, and key turning points in my life as I remember them. I have attempted to intermix factual information with episodes that are interesting to the reader. Additionally, I have stated candidly things that I consider important in life.

The book is not a genealogy. However, the opening chapter does give a brief narrative on some of my ancestors and my parents. Following that, the book basically covers important aspects of my personal life; i.e. actions of my parents, my birth and growing years, my family and its growth, and my career as an engineer.

My family has been most important to me. But to give the book some focus, I have purposely not given a lot of detail about members of my family or relatives. That would be another story. Thus, this book is not intended to be a family history. This is a book about me and written in the first person for the most part.

I have given only enough detail about my work at Pacific Gas & Electric Company to emphasize the broad experience base and the long years of service I had acquired, before I was found suitable for top level positions.

Again, I have stayed away from mentioning names of many work associates and their impact on my life because I did not want to stray away from my central theme.

As I wrote the various episodes of the book, I had a constant struggle with myself, because I wasn't including enough of my wife Alicia's contributions in the various family and career activities. Her contributions were immense. But I really would have gotten away from the subject matter if I had digressed to write about her. I know she understands. Nevertheless, Alicia, who I call "My Tucumcari Gal", has been at my side for over 43 years now and I thank her for being a part of me. My good fortune in meeting and marrying Alicia was the single most important event in my life. God was good to me in this regard.

Finally, like all the struggles in my life, it wasn't easy for me to write this book. But I enjoyed doing it. I found it to be a challenging and rewarding experience. For example, my spirits were lifted, and pride in my heritage was rekindled, when I recounted the stories about my mother and father. Their indominable faith in themselves and in God, and their courage, dignity, and love of family, are traits that should serve as a model for all our family and those that come after us.

Sincerely,

Jess R. Herrera
January 1, 1992
San Francisco, California

1
Family History
Ancestors and Parents

FATHER - ALBINO HERRERA AND HIS PARENTAGE

My father, Albino Herrera, was born in Central Spain (city unknown) on March 1, 1886. Practically no information about his family background or ancestry is available. However, older members of my family have told me that Albino's ancestors had some French lineage, in addition to their main Spanish heritage. Albino's father was named Francisco Herrera, but I have not been able to find out the name of Albino's mother. No other personal history is known about any other member of my father's ancestors.

However, it is a fact that the Herrera family emmigrated to Mexico when Albino was a very small boy. The reason for the family leaving their homeland and making the long and difficult journey across the Atlantic Ocean is not known, but one can only surmise that it was probably in an effort to improve their economic life. Historically we know that Western Europe was in the throes of a severe economic depression during the latter part of the 19th century. Also Spain itself had a lot of internal political strife and populance unrest during this period. But whatever the reason for emmigrating, it is obvious that it took a lot of courage and spirit of adventure for my father's family to make the trip from Spain and resettle in Mexico.

The Herrera family settled in Sain Alto, which is a small town in central west Mexico in the State of Zacatecas. Sain Alto has a population of less than 5,000 inhabitants. The town is located near Mexico Highway 45 and is about halfway between the capital city of Zacatecas, State of Zacatecas, and the capital city of Durango, State of Durango. Actually the closest town of any size to Sain Alto, is Fresnillo, which is about 35 miles to the south with a population of about 40,000 people. According to maps, Sain Alto is on the eastern slopes of the Sierra Madre Occidental mountain range and near the Continental Divide. The elevation is about 7500 feet in this area.

I do not know why the Herrera family settled deep in the interior of Mexico, rather than in more accessible regions of the country. One reason might be that work opportunities were available in that area at that particular time. This region of Mexico has long been famous as a center for mining silver, iron, and gold, and it also has vast agricultural farm lands and cattle ranges. Furthermore, it is interesting to note that the city of Durango which is the capital of the State of Durango, was founded in 1563 and named for Durango, Spain, a Basque town and home of its founder, Don Francisco de Ibarra. Perhaps my father's family knew about this area's cultural ties to Spain and so centuries later, decided to go to this region of Mexico where other Spanish people had previously settled. However these reasons are only guesses on my part.

Nevertheless, after they emmigrated to Mexico, Albino's parents and other family members, lived, raised their families, and presumably eventually died in Mexico.

MOTHER - SIMONA (RAMIREZ) HERRERA AND HER PARENTAGE

My mother's maiden name was Simona Ramirez. Her ancestry can be traced back as far as her paternal grandparents and her maternal great grandparents. These ancestors were all born in Mexico in the Sain Alto area, State of Zacatecas. Simona's paternal grandfather, Sebastian Ramirez, was born in 1836 and died in 1911. Sebastian married a woman named Maria Refugio Calderon, who was born in 1838. They gave birth to four boys and two girls. One of the sons was named Margarito Ramirez, my grandfather, who was born on June 3, 1862 in Sain Alto, Zacatecas, and died in El Paso, Texas on July 14, 1921.

The other pair of Simona's grandparents on her mother's side were Jose Maria Morales, who was born in 1832, and died in 1889, and Estanislada Andrade, who was born in 1841, and died in 1910. This latter couple's marriage resulted in a family consisting of two boys and five girls. One of the daughters from this union was named Francisca Morales, my grandmother, who was born in 1866, in Sain Alto, Zacatecas. To complete the record on Simona's great grandparents, Jose Maria Morales' parents were Juan Morales and Maria Trinidad Chaires. Also Estanislada Andrade's parents were Edwardo Andrade and

Maria de los Angeles Canales. A simplified ancestral chart is included in the Appendix to clarify the above lineage.

Margarito Ramirez and Francisca Morales, (my mother's parents), were married in Sain Alto, Zacatecas, Mexico, approximately in the year 1887. Very little is known about their early life. However they did start a family which eventually lead to three sons and three daughters. The family consisted of Daniel, who was born in 1888; Maria, born on March 22, 1890; Antonia, born in 1893; Simona (my mother), born on March 25, 1897; Francisco, born in 1906; and Manuel who was born in 1916 (approximate date). All these children were born and raised in Sain Alto, Zacatecas.

ALBINO AND SIMONA MARRY

Of the six Ramirez' offspring only two of the daughters, Simona and Maria, subsequently were married. Since my father, Albino had grown up and lived in Sain Alto, he had known Simona (my mother) since she was quite young. He had watched her grow up and when Simona became of age, Albino asked for her hand in marriage. Simona's parents thought this would be a good match for their daughter, even though Albino was 11 years older than Simona. This age disparity was not unusual for those times. So Simona Ramirez and Albino Herrera were married in the Catholic Church in Sain Alto, Zacatecas in the year 1914. At that time Albino, my father, was 28 years of age and Simona, my mother, was 17 years young.

Maria, the oldest Ramirez daughter, had married a few years earlier in the year 1910, to a man named Luis Flores. They also were married in the Catholic Church in Sain Alto. This marriage eventually resulted in nine children. I should note that in later years I was very close to, and grew up with, some of these cousins.

The Ramirez family and the Herrera and Flores couples, eventually moved north to the Gomez Palacio - Torreon area of Mexico, and some members actually lived in a small town near this area called Velardeña. Velardeña is important in the history of our family because this is where my parents (Albino and Simona) eventually settled and started their family. Velardeña is in the State of Durango and is a very small town of less than 2500 inhabitants. It is located in the central northeast section of the state and about 52 miles south of the large important city of Gomez Palacio and near the border of the State of Coahuila and it's large city of Torreon. The distance from Sain Alto, Zacatecas to Velardeña is between 110 and 130 road miles depending on the route one takes.

So it is noted that these family ancestors actually moved north, a distance of roughly 160 miles, from their ancestral home in Sain Alto to the Gomez Palacio area to continue their lives. This resettlement occurred in the year 1914 (approximate date) just after the marriage of my parents. Again one can only guess at the reasons for moving this great distance (for those times), but it was probably to find work for the men of the family. Also the family was very close and all moved together, or within a very short time span. Additionally, it is known that during this period the Mexican Revolution was in full swing, so the general populance was in a state of severe stress and unrest, which I'm sure affected these ancestors in many ways. This included such hardships as poor economic conditions, civil unrest, religious persecution, personal harassment, and work uncertainty.

EARLY MARRIED LIFE - ALBINO AND SIMONA HERRERA

My parents, Albino and Simona Herrera, settled in Velardeña, Durango, where Albino owned and operated a small grocery store. They were considered poor, but at this time of their lives they at least managed to earn a living by this means. Albino was quite resourceful, intelligent, and hardworking and he had a formal but limited school education. He knew how to read and write. He was a man of high moral standards and of good character and with no apparent vices or bad habits. He was very gentle and good hearted by nature, but some thought him to be a quiet man and reserved in his mannerisms. Albino was a man of medium stature; about 5'-6" tall and 150 pounds in weight. He was of medium (not dark) complexion and with black hair and brown deep-set eyes. As was the custom in those days for men, he wore a short mustache.

Simona was an attractive young woman about 5'-6" in height and about 125 pounds in weight. She was of medium complexion; a shade darker than her husband's. Her hair was long, and dark black in color. Her big brown eyes were deep set in a face with striking high cheek bones. Her lips were medium full and her mouth was average in size. Simona also had a formal but limited school education, and she knew how to read and write (in Spanish) quite well.

Simona was brought up by her parents to be a deeply religious Catholic and because of this, she was a person with high moral standards and a deep love for other members of her family. She learned at an early age to be a hardworking person. Since she came from a large poor family, everyone had to pitch in and do their share in order to help their parents make ends meet. Simona's temperament was always calm and under control, yet she could be quite forceful at times. She was a woman of high energy and high spirit, and everyone liked her because of her outgoing, yet pleasant, personality.

Soon after Albino and Simona Herrera settled into their married life in the town of Velardeña they wanted to start a family and sure enough, they did. Two days after Christmas on December 27, 1915, their first baby was born. It was a daughter and they named her Juanita. The whole family rejoiced and this blessed event was the occasion for a big celebration among the family and their friends. Juanita was baptized soon thereafter. Another reason for this celebration was to ease the family grieving due to the death of my mother's older sister Antonia, who had died on September 7, 1914 at age 21. This sister died of peritonitis after a sickness that lasted only four days. The family had felt very bad about Antonia's death and so the birth of a brand new baby was a happy occasion for all.

For the next two years during 1916 and 1917, the Ramirez, Herrera and Flores families continued to try to carry on their lives in Velardeña and in Gomez-Palacio, Durango. However, because of the generally poor economic conditions in Mexico during this time, the families had a hard time making ends meet. And even though the Mexican revolution was historically in its latter stages, the effects of the constant strife on the working people of Mexico was devastating and disturbing. Most people, including my ancestors, were sympathetic to the aims of the Mexican Revolution, and in fact supported it. Nevertheless, the turmoil and unrest was quite a heavy burden and certainly did not improve the people's living conditions; in fact the opposite was happening at that particular time. As it turned out, the Mexican Revolution had a large impact on the history of our family.

MEXICAN REVOLUTION - 1910 TO 1920

Perhaps in order to get a better perspective on the conditions in Mexico during this time, a brief historical summary would help:

Mexico's beginnings as an independent nation were in 1821 when she cut her last ties with Spain. However, history tells us that Mexicans were not prepared to rule their own nation. They did not have any self-rule experience and under Spanish rule they were left with the general masses of people in general poverty and illiterate. So for the next 100 years Mexico had much civil strife as leaders with varying ideological theories ruled the nation. If we skip past the eras of Santa Anna, Benito Juarez, and Porfirio Diaz, this brings us to the more modern period when the Mexican Revolution took place.

This period, between the years 1910 to 1920, was one of great turmoil in the history of Mexico. The year 1910 introduced a terrifying decade in which the nation was torn from end to end and new leaders, pursued their visions or their ambitions. Francisco Madero in 1911, Victoriano Huerta in 1913, and Venustiano Carranza in 1914, were successive presidents who tried to bring the various idealogical factions together, but to no avail.

The rival factions were headed up by Emiliano Zapata, Pancho Villa, and Alvaro Obregon. Each of these men, and Carranza, in effect had control of different regions of Mexico. Furthermore, their armies, and followers roamed the lands fighting, killing, burning, looting, and wrecking, all for causes which they apparently deemed necessary to correct the social evils of the land. The result was, however, that many political and social ills continued to be piled on this unhappy land and it's people.

Carranza, as president in 1917, held a Constitutional Convention and enunciated a revolutionary doctrine that had far reaching implications. The new laws were very strict and affected the Church, domestic and foreign owners of business and property, labor laws, and the general populance in many ways. Nevertheless, by 1919, Carranza's power was slipping and the land was still in anarchy. Carranza was murdered in 1920 and replaced by Obregon. Thus, this turbulent phase of the Mexican Revolution ended in 1920.

FAMILY EMMIGRATION TO THE UNITED STATES

Considering the generally unstable conditions in Mexico as described above, one can certainly imagine how difficult it must of been for my ancestors and parents to carry on anything resembling a normal life. Furthermore, the men of the family were under constant threat of being conscripted into either Carranza's or Pancho Villa's guerrilla forces. So after much deliberation and with much anguish, the family decided to try for a better life by leaving Mexico, their homeland, and emmigrating to the United States.

Therefore, during the latter part of 1917 the Ramirez family and the Flores family travelled together by train from their homes in central Mexico to El Paso, Texas, which was their destination. This was a distance of almost 600 miles via Chihuahua City, Mexico. They stopped for a short time in Cuidad Juarez, at the Mexico - United States border, in order to obtain their passports. The Ramirez family consisted of my grandmother Francisca, grandfather Margarito, and their three sons, Daniel, Francisco, and Manuel. The Flores family consisted of my aunt Maria, and her husband Luis, and their two small children.

My parents, Simona and Albino, stayed behind in Mexico for a few months in order to dispose of their small grocery shop. Later, the Herrera family left Velardeña, Mexico in early 1918, got their passports in Cuidad Juarez, Mexico and joined the rest of the family in El Paso, Texas. Juanita Herrera, their only daughter, was 2 years old when this trip was taken. However, my parents were expecting their second child at this time. Subsequently, upon it's birth on June 13, 1918, in El Paso, Texas, this baby was the first offspring of our entire ancestral family to be born as a United State citizen. This second child born to my parents, was a girl and they named her Antonia (they called her Tonia), in honor of a favorite patron saint of theirs, Saint Anthony of Padua. Tonia was baptized in Sacred Heart Catholic Church.

My parents now had two daughters in the Herrera family. Furthermore, they were now about to start another phase of their lives, and in a strange land. Their courage and faith in God was what kept them going and gave them hope. At this stage of their lives Albino, my father, was 32 years old (he was to live only 10 years longer), and my mother, Simona, was 21 years old. They had been married for only four years.

THE HERRERA FAMILY IN EL PASO, TEXAS; 1918 - 1923

Shortly after arriving in El Paso, Texas, my grandmother, Francisca Ramirez, and grandfather, Margarito Ramirez, were able to buy a small cottage at 803 South St. Vrain Street. This was an area of town where only Mexican descent people lived in the "barrios". This district, by any standards, was the poor section of town. Living with my grandparents at the time were their three sons; Daniel (age 30), Francisco (age 12), and Manuel (age 2). They eked out a living with Margarito and Daniel working as construction laborers using adobe and other earthwork materials.

The Flores family rented a small home on South Tays Street right next to the United States - Mexican border and the Rio Grande River. This district was in the 2nd Ward barrio of South El Paso. Luis Flores, my uncle, who was a very hard working man, started out as a laborer and doing other odd jobs. All in all, however, the living conditions had started out rather bleakly for the Ramirez and Flores families in El Paso.

When my parents got to El Paso in March, 1918, my father, Albino, had a difficult time finding work of any kind. For about six months he worked at temporary jobs, but their savings were being used up. So in early September he decided to take a drastic step. He signed up with a labor broker who transported him, and others, over a thousand miles away, to the lumber mills in northern Oregon to work there. He went alone on this daring adventure hoping to earn some money so that he could soon have his wife, Simona, and their two children join him. As an alien, (World War 1 was still ongoing) the records show that he presented himself to the authorities in Oregon, as required by law, on September 12, 1918. This was in the town of Maupia, Wasco County, Oregon. This town is near The Dalles, Oregon.

Albino was in Oregon for about six months. However the working conditions were very hard and as a commercial man, occupation wise, he was not used to working with his hands as a laborer. Also, he yearned to be back with his family. He had sent most of the money he had earned back to his family, but with the money he had left he decided to return to El Paso in early 1919. Even though he was disappointed that the Oregon adventure had not provided prospects for a permanent home base for the Herrera family in the Northwest, he was happy to rejoin his family. After returning to El Paso, Albino decided to try a more familiar way for him to make a living, i.e. as a merchant.

In El Paso, my parents lived in a rented small house on South St. Vrain Street in the 2nd Ward barrio district. Albino's prior experience was as a commercial man, so with what was left of their savings my parents opened up a small grocery store in south El Paso called "El Cuatro de Julio". (This tranlates to "The 4th of July"). The name had nothing to do with the U.S. Independence day; it simply reflected the day and month the store opened for business in 1919. Most of the goods to stock the store were bought across the border in Juarez, Mexico. The proceeds from this business were meager but at least my parents were able to eke out a living by this means; so life went on.

In May 1921, Albino and Simona, my parents, had another baby girl. This was their third and they named her Maria de la Luz Herrera. They were quite happy about this, as the baby was healthy and this event raised the spirits of the whole family. However soon after that, their joy turned to mourning because my mother's father, Margarito Ramirez passed away. This occurred at four o'clock in the afternoon on Friday, July 14, 1921. He was 59 years of age. He died after a long infectious illness that had persisted for about two years; with the last two months in great pain. Margarito died and was buried in El Paso. As the result of this death, my grandmother, Francisca Ramirez, was now a widow but at least her three sons were still living. Daniel, the oldest, undertook to provide the financial support for the Ramirez family.

After the above mentioned major events, life in El Paso during the ensuing period was fairly routine for my parents. They were simple hardworking folks and of happy disposition and good humor. Albino and Simona took great pleasure in visiting with relatives and had numerous family gatherings with lively conversation and good home cooked Mexican food. They attended Sacred Heart Catholic Church in their neighborhood which allowed them to practice their faith and nourish their love for the Lord. Also, they were able to meet other people at Sunday Mass. Juanita, had started going to the local public school about this time also.

Generally however, life was still hard economically for those who lived in the barrios. Even though economic conditions in the United States were getting better after World War 1, the effects of this improvement were not felt in the El Paso barrios. The slum conditions and job situation did not improve much, if any, for the people of Mexican descent. My father's customers in the area were all quite poor. He was forced to extend credit to many of his customers for goods purchased, and many folks simply could not repay him. As a matter of fact his "goodness" and genuine concern for those less fortunate then him resulted in his barely making a meager profit. He did not have much to show for his investment and long hours spent at the store.

Soon thereafter, another tragedy struck the Herrera family. Maria de la Luz, baby Lucita as she was called, caught the measles, developed intestinal problems with high fever, plus pneumonia like complications. The sickness and infections came on and spread suddenly, and the doctors at El Paso General Hospital Clinic could not arrest the fever. After being sick for about one and a half months the baby died. This was on Holy Thursday, March 19, 1923. She was not quite two years old.

My parents were devastated and quite sad about this cruel turn of events. They loved their small baby so much, and Juanita and Antonia had been having lots of fun playing with their sister, Lucita. Nevertheless, even as they mourned the loss of their baby, the Herreras consoled each other and pressed on with their lives. But somehow, in spite of their determination and perseverance, life in the United States was not working out for the Herreras as well as they had hoped.

My father and mother were not about to give up however, as they were still young and optimistic by nature; also they believed quite strongly that the Will of God was being done. They resolved to find a way out of the hopelessness of their situation. They especially needed to find a way to provide them with more income as it was hard to make ends meet. They decided that if Simona could run the store, even with two small children to take care of, then my father could get another job and thus help their financial situation.

In looking around for another job, Albino found out through the immigration office that the lumber industry in Northern California was offering employment for workers. Also they advertised that housing and facilities, including schools, were available for families. Since Albino already had a taste for this kind of work earlier in Oregon, he thought that if he could take his family with him, things would be better for him this time. But he still faced the hurdle of convincing his wife that this was a good move. After about a month's time and after a lot of discussion, Simona and Albino made a big decision.

HERRERA FAMILY RELOCATES AGAIN - 1923

Once again my parents, Albino and Simona, decided to uproot their lives and travel elsewhere to seek a better life for themselves and their family. They decided that they would cast their hopes for the future in the lumber camps of Northern California. For Simona, the most painful thing she had to endure was the separation from her mother and family relatives. She loved them dearly, but being a resourceful woman, deep down she knew that she had to suffer through this and sacrifice her true feelings for the future good of her immediate family. As a matter of fact, she even tried to talk her mother and other members of the Ramirez and Flores families to leave El Paso with them, but they would not. They did not want to jeopardize their basically secure life in El Paso, even if life there was hard.

So in late June, 1923, my parents spent the last of what little money they had, for railroad tickets, and with their two children, took the train and set out for a place in Northern California in Lassen County, called Westwood. You can't say that they "moved" there, because what few possessions they took were in two large suitcases. (Later on, my grandmother sent a trunkful of their other belongings, such as bedding, kitchen ware, clothes, and nicnaks).

One can only wonder at the fear and uncertainty that my parents felt as they undertook a journey of over 1400 miles from El Paso, Texas to the forested wilderness of Westwood, California. What future awaited them there? My mother Simona, was particularly concerned. How was she going to cope without the daily support of her mother Francisca, and older sister Maria? To add to her apprehension, she had just found out that month that she was pregnant once again. How was she going to deliver her baby with no woman friends nearby? Also she had heard that the climate in Northern California was quite severe, with lots of snow and very cold winters; this would be quite a change from the dry arid climate of El Paso.

As I think about this trek, I marvel at the great courage of a couple of individuals who just a few years previous had left their homeland in Mexico. They were now pressing forward in these United States in the true pioneering spirit.

Juanita, was almost eight years old at that time and Antonia was about five. The two girls took the four day trip in stride. They thoroughly enjoyed the trainride and did not seem to mind the endless delays at the various stops and transfer points. To them it was all a great adventure and they seemingly were waiting to make new friends in a strange land. After a long and tiring traintrip through towns and cities that seemed very strange to them, the last part of the journey was by bus from Sacramento, California. The Herrera family arrived in Westwood on June 30, 1923.

My father's pioneering spirit was still dominant. He had come from Spain, crossed the Atlantic Ocean, settled and lived in various towns and cities in Mexico, emmigrated to the United States and settled in El Paso, Texas, worked in Oregon, and now was starting a new life in the northern forests of California, in a place called Westwood. This quiet, determined man hoped and prayed that with God's help, the Herrera family would find a happy life in this new location.

2
Early Childhood Years

WESTWOOD, CALIFORNIA

The town of Westwood, California is in Lassen County in the Northeastern part of the State at the southern end of the Cascade Mountain Range. The elevation there is 5,113 feet. The town was founded by the Walker family in 1912 as the center for it's Red River Lumber Company operations in Northern California. The Appendix of this writing gives a brief history of Westwood and relates how it became the center for an extensive lumber industry in California. The story of Westwood is truly an interesting saga of a unique town which was started from scratch and then operated for over 40 years, and how its inhabitants survived the ups and downs of the lumber industry. I recommend referral to this section of the Appendix in order to capture for the reader, the concept of the paternalistic "company town", which no longer exists in America today.

Westwood was a "company town" in the sense that all facilities in the town were owned and operated by the Walker family through their Red River Lumber Company. When I say they owned everything in town, that's what I mean. There was no private ownership of businesses nor property. The sole industry in the town was lumbering; this included the mill in town, as well as the logging operations in the nearby forests.

One of the main attributes of the town was the houses that were built for the workers and their families. These houses were all built of wood, and in the early 1920's were rented out to the workers for from $10 to $21 per month. The streets were laid at right angles to each other and alphabetically named after trees; i.e. Ash (A), Birch (B), Cedar (C), etc. The perpendicular streets were numbered; i.e. First, Second, Third, etc. Only one or two of these streets were paved and had wooden sidewalks alongside them. The remainder of the streets were just dirt roads.

A few other prominent buildings were also in the town. These included the mill itself, a hospital, a grammar school, a high school (built in 1927), a large department store which included a grocery section, a theatre, Catholic and Baptist churches, the firehouse, a pool hall, and various other municipal and Company administration buildings. The whole main town of Westwood took up an area of only about one square mile; however two adjacent smaller sized areas also existed where people lived. These other less desirable areas (actually slums) were Old Town and Robbers Creek. The people who lived in these two areas were mostly foreign-born poorer people who couldn't afford to live in the main part of town. These people were of Mexican, Spanish, Italian, Greek, and Armenian ancestry, as well as a very few American Indians.

FAMILY IN WESTWOOD

Upon arrival in Westwood in June, 1923, the Herrera family adjusted to life as quickly as they could. My father, Albino, was soon hired by the Red River Lumber Company as a laborer in the sawmill. He worked at the mill handling the cut lumber as it came off of the large circular saw assembly lines. At times he also handled the logs and directed them into the spinning saws. The work was dangerous, quite tiring, and very labor intensive. For his efforts he was paid the average wage for laborers, which was about $12 for a six-day work week. The family managed to subsist on this amount as both my mother and father were frugal in their living habits. One thing that helped was that the Company provided complete medical care for each worker and his family for only $1.00 per month; this included hospital care, if needed.

My family lived in a two bedroom wood frame Company house at 621 Cedar Street. The rent was $17 per month. Our house had an inside toilet and water faucet, as well as a wood burning stove and heater for cooking and keeping warm. Also, the house had a few indoor electrical lights, for which the charge was 25 cents per month per lightbulb. Most of the money earned went for rent and food, however that first year, relatively large sums were spent to buy a few house furnishings. My mother was a good seamstress and made most of the clothes for the family. The material was bought from the Sears-Roebuck or Montgomery-Ward catalogs. This was done furtively, as workers were expected to buy their goods at the Company store. Additionally, Simona frequently received some material and other staples from her mother and sister in El Paso via the United States mail. This helped a lot.

Since Westwood was a small close community, my parents soon made friends with three other Mexican families; the Gonzalez, Perez, and the Campos. Each of these families talked Spanish of course, were Catholic, and had small children, so getting together from time to time and socializing was a welcome change from the everyday routines. These families were very religious and practiced their faith. They attended Mass and other services at Our Lady Of The Snows Catholic Church in Westwood; during this period, a visiting priest from Susanville came to Westwood every Sunday for two masses, and to administer other Sacramental functions. So all in all, the Herrera family was adapting to this changed life in the Northern woods. In the Fall of 1923, Juanita started school in the third grade, and Antonia started kindergarten. The girls were happy about this because it allowed them to make new friends. Also, as it turned out, it was good for them to learn English, as Spanish was the spoken language at home.

That first winter in Westwood however, was a big test for every member of the young Herrera family. They had to come to grips with the harsh realities of the bitter cold and snow. They were not accustomed to this type of weather. The snow piled high by the houses by Christmas time; which made getting around, difficult and dangerous. The Company provided snow removal service on the streets but this still left a lot of snow everywhere else. The family learned the hard way about keeping warm, freezing water pipes, heavy clothing, influenza, shoveling snow, wet feet, slippery walkways, ice everywhere, heavy winds and blinding snow, being housebound, and a lot more inconveniences that they had never experienced before. Nevertheless, they were all determined to stick it out in Westwood; and their faith in God never wavered.

MY BIRTH

That winter, the Herrera family spirits were lifted because I was born on January 18, 1924, and became the first born boy of the family. I was born in the Westwood hospital and was a healthy baby boy with medium dark complexion and lots of black hair. I was named Jesus (after Jesus Christ), and was baptized two weeks later in Our Lady of the Snows Catholic Church in Westwood. The occasion was a happy one for the family and my parents had a celebration at the house with many of their close friends invited to partake in the festivities. With the help of her lady friends, my mother, Simona, prepared a traditional Mexican fiesta with delicious food, music, and a piñata party for the kids.

I was given the nickname "Chuy" in Spanish, and my sisters also called me by my English name, "Jesse or Jess". Albino was particularly proud of his first male offspring, as it meant that with God's help, the Herrera name could now be perpetuated into the future. So as the next year passed I grew and developed under the loving and expert care of my mother, father, and sisters.

The love between Albino and Simona continued to grow, and on June 21, 1925, a second boy was born into the family in Westwood. This boy was named Raimundo, (or Raymond, in English), and was called Rey (or Ray) for short. Ray was baptized into the Catholic faith soon therafter. By this time the Herrera family consisted of father, Albino, age 39; mother, Simona, age 28; two girls, Juanita, age 9, and Antonia, age 7; and two baby boys, Jess and Ray.

FAMILY LIFE

The following three years were full of pleasant memories for the Herrera family. Even though life in Westwood was hard at times, especially for my parents, the family learned to cope with their problems and settled down to making a decent living for themselves. By any standard the family was poor economically, but at least they had food and shelter and a good family life and a few close friends. Simona was the homemaker, Albino was the breadwinner, Juanita and Antonia were in school, and the two boys were growing by leaps and bounds. It should be noted that the relationship between my father and mother was one of complete harmony. They treated each other with respect; at no time were any harsh words spoken. It was obvious that Albino adored and loved his young wife. Also, it was understood that Albino was the head of the family. But at the same time, my mother was a forceful, intelligent woman and she contributed a lot towards the direction and conduct of the family doings.

Both parents demonstrated their love for their children. However, their approaches were quite different. Albino was more reserved in demeanor and never raised his voice, nevertheless he spent a lot of time playing with and talking to the chidren; they all loved and adored him because he was such a gentle man. Simona was more approachable and fun-loving, and displayed her affection outwardly for the children. But at the same time she was the disciplinarian; a look or a word from her was all that the children needed to correct their conduct. Also being at home, Simona was the "teacher" of the children. She taught them songs, games, crafts, writing, prayers, and how to do chores. Also she was a very good story teller.

MEMORIES OF A SMALL BOY

From the deep subconscious depths of my brain I remember quite vividly a few incidents from my early childhood. These give examples of how my parents showed their affection for me. At the time I was only about three to four years of age.

My brother Ray and I took my father's lunch to him at the mill, every workday. The hot lunch was prepared by my mother and consisted of the best food that the family could afford. Usually the lunch included beans, rice, meat, potatoes, tortillas, and some vegetables, fruit and cookies. The lunch was neatly packed by my mother into a black metal lunchpail with a handle. It was a hearty meal, but my father apparently needed this kind of sustenance because of the hard manual work that his job required. When we got to the mill, which was about three quarters of a mile from home, we waited for the mill lunch whistle to blow and then we would go through the gate and deliver our father's lunch to him.

We then had the option of returning home right away, or waiting around until my father finished his lunch. We always waited. We would play amongst the logs in the mill pond while my father ate his lunch. When the mill whistle blew again, signifying the end of the lunch period, Ray and I would then seek out my father, pick up the now empty lunchpail, and leave to go home. Once outside the mill gates, we would hurriedly open up the lunchpail to see if my father had left anything; sure enough and without fail, there would always be cookies or some fruit or some other goodie left in the lunchpail. Of course, Ray and I ate whatever was left and our stomachs felt very good as we skipped home. At the time I never could figure out why it was that my father always left the best part of his lunch uneaten!

On another occasion, my mother sent Ray and I to the store with a dime to buy a loaf of bread. As we meandered along the wooden sidewalk, the dime fell out of my hand and dropped through the cracks of the sidewalk boards and down to the ground below. This was a catastrophe because there was no way for us to retrieve the money even though we tried everything we could think of. I was terrified at what my mother would say about my clumsiness and the loss of this "great amount" of money; so I started to cry, and then Ray started to cry. After a slow torturous walk home, we entered the house still crying, and told mother our sad tale of woe.

I can still remember what happened next: She took both of us onto her lap, hugged us, and told us not to worry. She said she had thought about baking some homemade bread anyway, so if we would help her do that, she would have the bread baked before father got home for the evening meal. I can not express in words my relief and joy at this happy ending - it meant that my mother was not mad at me, nor were we going to be punished in any way. However, I will say that I learned a lesson; from then on anytime I was sent on an errand with money, the money was kept in my pocket until I got to the store counter.

Another memory I have of my loving father was his gathering me onto his knee and counseling me not to fight with my younger brother Ray. The kind, gentle way that he reprimanded me upon that occasion left a lasting impression on me, up to the present.

So life in Westwood went on for us, and in January, 1928 another blessed event occurred in the family. My mother gave birth to another baby girl. She was named Amalia. Again, the family rejoiced when this happened, and the girls Juanita and Antonia, especially were happy to have a little baby sister that they could play with and help take care of. Seemingly, our lives in Westwood had settled down and my father's dreams of a good life for his family in a place far removed from his origins were being fulfilled. He was happy.

FATHER'S DEATH

A few months later our tranquil family life was shattered and resulted in tragedy for the family! It all started in early March, 1928 when my father got sick with influenza. The doctors at the hospital could not find the right medication to combat the viral infection and his sickness continued throughout the months of April, May, and early June. To make matters worse, on June 5th my mother, Simona, started to get sick from severe head and neck pain attacks which lasted from 5 to 10 minutes each. During the ensuing days, she eventually lost consciousness and the last Catholic rites and Holy Sacraments were prayed over her. She revived and was then taken to the Susanville General Hospital where she was in the intensive care ward under observation. She was there for four days.

During all this time, there was no one to take care of all the children so my grandmother, Francisca, (we called her "Quica"), came from El Paso to help out. The trip was difficult for her because she was 62 years of age by then.

Quica arrived on June 14th in Susanville. My mother was by then feeling better so the doctors allowed her to return to Westwood with Quica.

In the meantime my father, who had been praying to God to give his wife life, took a turn for the worst from his continuing sickness. On June 8th he developed pneumonia and was taken to the Westwood Hospital. However with no adequate infection fighting drugs or medication available in those days, my father continued to suffer. By June 15th he was critically ill and was hemorrhaging badly. With my grandmother, my mother, and my two older sisters at his bedside, my father, Albino Herrera died in the Westwood Hospital on Saturday, June 16, 1928 at three o'clock in the afternoon. He was 42 years of age. He left a family of five children and his wife; Simona his beloved wife was 31 years of age, Juanita, the oldest daughter was 12, Antonia, another daughter was 10, the two boys, Jess and Ray, were 4 and 3 respectively, and a baby girl Amalia was 5 months old.

It should be noted that Albino's death certificate as signed by Jay Jacobs M.D. indicates the cause of death as "tuberculosis lungs."

Albino was buried in Westwood Cemetery on the 18th day of June, 1928 at 2:30 o'clock in the afternoon, with Father McCarthy from the Lady of the Snows Catholic Church conducting the service. Many of his friends and all his family attended the funeral. I remember very vividly the lowering of the casket into the grave. A beautiful gravestone made of granite was later placed by my mother at her husband's grave. It is in the form of a cross with the following inscription in Spanish: "Albino Herrera Murio el 16 de Junio de 1928 ala Edad de 42 Anos, Su Esposa y

Hijos Dedican este Recuerdo."

FAMILY LIFE WORSENS

The loss of a beloved husband and father was a devastating setback to the Herrera family. Everyone was grief stricken and very sad to realize that such a good person was no longer around to provide protection, stability, companionship, and love to their everyday lives. Also, the harsh, practical realities of her husband's death was of great worry and concern to Simona. Chief among these thoughts was that she was now left with five young children and providing for their material support was going to be very difficult.

Grandmother Quica tried to talk Simona into leaving Westwood, together with the children, and returning to El Paso to live with the rest of the Ramirez family. However Simona did not want to do this; she rationalized that her children would have a better education and life in Westwood than in the "barrios" of El Paso. She did not know how she was going to survive without her husband, but she placed her trust in the Lord and vowed that she would work hard to keep her family intact. So my grandmother, Quica, reluctantly returned to El Paso by herself. But she extracted a promise that in the near future my mother would reconsider her decision and return to El Paso with her children, if things did not work out well for them in Westwood. As it turned out, the next few years did in fact prove to be very difficult ones, especially for my mother.

The next setback was the unexpected death of my baby sister, Amalia. She died on November 30, 1928 as the result of childhood measles, coupled with an influenza type sickness. At the time, Amalia was only ten months of age. She was buried alongside her father Albino, in Westwood cemetery, on December 2nd. This death was a sad event, especially for the Herrera children, since they soon realized that they did not have their happy baby sister to play with anymore. However, life went on.

The Herrera family continued to live on Cedar Street as my mother, Simona, managed to support herself and her family. She did this by washing and ironing clothes for several of the single and transient men who worked in the mill. Also, from time to time she sold material dry goods, such as shirts, that her mother bought in Juarez, Mexico and sent to her. Additionally, she had several very close Mexican-American friends and families, who gave Simona a lot of both material help and moral/social support. Since my mother was very popular in this community of friends, they practically considered the Herreras as an extension of their own families.

However from an economic standpoint, life in Westwood for all inhabitants soon turned worse. This was because of the stock market crash of October, 1929 and the severe economic depression that followed in the United States. The Red River Lumber Company tried mightily to ride through the lumber business turndown and did manage to keep the mill operating on a reduced capacity basis well into 1930. Economically, the situation for Simona and her young family was starting to get desperate. Money was quite scarce and wages were being reduced for the workers, which in turn made it tough for Simona to make ends meet and satisfy creditors. Simona now had to make a major decision regarding the family future once again. Was now the time to leave Westwood and return to El Paso?

3
The Great Depression Years

MY MOTHER STRUGGLES

Despite the bad economic times in Westwood in the year 1930, Simona thought that with God's help she could still manage to survive and keep her family in Westwood. Juanita (or Janie as we called her) was to start high school in the fall of 1930, and Simona was determined that all her children get the best education possible and even go to college. She believed the chances to do this would be better in Westwood and Northern California than in the Southwest city of El Paso. Besides, her mother in El Paso had recently written to her and related that the economic situation for Mexican - Americans there was very bad. Unemployment, poverty, and racial prejudice was present, especially for those unfortunate Chicanos who lived in the "barrios". So despite the longing to be with her blood family during those hard times, Simona chose to stay in Westwood for a while longer to see how things would go for herself and her family.

As time went on, through acquaintances, she met a young man named Ricardo Morales. What happened next was unexpected. Morales took a liking to Simona and soon tried to talk her into having an affair with him. While this man was good to her, Simona did not love him and certainly had no thoughts of remarrying, especially so soon after Albino's death. Nevertheless, and for whatever reason, she sacrificed her innermost feelings and agreed.

In October 1930, after knowing Morales for only a very short time, Simona became pregnant. Upon becoming aware of this development, Morales left Westwood and did not return. It is rumored that he returned to his native land of Mexico. I do not know why he left, but I surmise that it was partly because he did not want to get involved with any family responsibility. Simona did not immediately tell her mother or other family members in El Paso about her pregnancy, because she felt they would not understand the situation and would chastise her for what had happened.

However, Simona placed her trust in the Lord and because of her faith, knew that she could depend on God's help. An example of this was a letter that Simona wrote in December, 1930 to her ailing younger brother, Francisco, who was in El Paso, Texas (See Appendix). In this very poignant letter she asked Francisco to pray to the Blessed Virgin that she be granted a special personal favor upon which "the well being of her children depended." I can only guess that my mother was concerned about the successful birth of her new baby, as well as about her continued ability to support her young family.

Anyone who reads this letter can sense and feel what a pious, God loving person my mother was. And even though Simona's life was still a tough struggle she was not about to give up in despair, nor wallow in self pity. In fact the main purpose of the letter was to lift the spirits of her brother Francisco, who was chronically ill with tuberculosis. Another key revelation that indicated what my mother was thinking about at that time, was her plan to only remain in Westwood until Janie graduated from high school. Following that, the family would then all go to El Paso to live.

The above referenced hand written letter in Spanish is a family treasure. I have included the translation in the Appendix. I urge everyone to read it.

ANOTHER SISTER BORN

On July 2, 1931, at the height of the "Great Depression" in America, my sister Isobel Guadalupe, was born in Westwood, California. Soon thereafter, on July 20, 1931 she was baptized in The Lady of the Snows Catholic Church in Westwood by the Reverend Michael O'Connell. Marcelino and Mary Avila, a married couple who were one of Simona's closest friends were the "padrinos" (sponsors). It should be noted that despite being fathered by Ricardo Morales, Isobel's baptismal certificate indicates her last name as "Herrera". This was as Simona wanted it.

For Janie, Tonia, Jess and Ray, there was rejoicing because once again, they had a beautiful baby sister in the family. In Simona's and the childrens' minds Isobel was replacing the baby girl, Amalia, whom the family had lost just a short time ago. Because of this, they all got down on their knees and gave thanks to God. Also at this time, Simona notified her mother and her sister in El Paso about the new baby. As it turned out, all in the family there were also thrilled about this blessed event; my mother was overjoyed and quite relieved.

However, my mother's trials and hardships were not over. She was still left with the burden of supporting a growing family by her own wits and courage. To add to her concerns, Simona was heartbroken to learn that on August 12, 1931, her younger brother Francisco, whom she loved dearly, had died in El Paso at age 25. Francisco was buried in Evergreen cemetery in El Paso, Texas. Simona's older brother, Daniel, had previously died on December 14, 1926 in El Paso at age 38, after a long bout with severe pneumonia. Simona felt bad for her mother, Quica, because the two sons that had lived with her and taken good care of her were now gone.

So all in all, the events of the past three years had been major tests of Simona's indominable spirit and her faith in God. However, she possessed a strong inner fiber and character that made her all the more determined to press forward and carry on, in spite of continued adversity. The Spirit of the Holy Ghost was certainly within her! She continued to believe that His will was being done.

NO. 4 ROBBERS CREEK

Simona's immediate concern was to somehow find a way to support herself and her five growing children during those bad economic times in Westwood. One of the first things that she and her family did was to move out of the Company house on Cedar Street. They could no longer afford to pay the rent there. So Simona purchased a small cabin at No. 4 Robbers Creek, which was on the outskirts of town, for $100. This was on October 31, 1931. The terms of the sale included a $50 down payment, and with the remaining amount to be paid in installments at an interest rate of 1% per annum. I don't know how my mother got the $50 down payment, but it took her six months to pay off the total contract amount and get title to the house.

The word "house" is used loosely here. It was small, in bad shape structurally and in need of major repair. The house was on a large level rock filled lot, it had a lean-to woodshed adjacent to the house itself, and of course there was an outhouse in the back of the lot. It wasn't much more than a cabin, but my mother was determined that this was to be our home, since it was all she could afford.

With the expert help of Señor Campos, who was a carpenter and a good family friend, the house was soon repaired and made habitable. Additionally, an enclosed porch was added which served as a bedroom for the two older girls. Also, in time a new roof and new siding were installed, and inside improvements were made. The reason this sticks out in my mind is that for many months the whole family pitched in to work and help with the repairs. I remember quite vividly wrestling with the new roof rafters, nailing roof shingles and siding boards, and cutting and carrying lumber for the various operations. At the end of the work day, Ray and I were too tired to even play. I was only about eight years old at the time and needless to say, I learned a lot about carpentry from this hard work experience.

WESTWOOD RECOLLECTIONS

It was during this time starting in 1932, that recollections of my personal and family life were most vivid. Life was hard for my mother but I was too young to realize just how hard it was.

Mother took in washing and ironed and mended shirts for the workers to earn a few pennies. Additionally she sold shirts, aprons, and tableclothes that she made from material sent to her by her mother. We sold candy to the neighborhood kids. It was always a temptation for me to see the boxes of Hersheys or Baby Ruths just sitting there on a chair by the front door; but of course I didn't dare to do more than just look. A box of candies cost my mother $0.80 and if all the box was sold she realized $1.20 (40 cents profit). Another "famous" money raising endeavor was the selling of "hot tamales"; but I'll get to that later.

In spite of the severe economic hardships that we endured, most of my memories during those times were quite pleasant. I was growing up and experiencing the fun of doing so. I guess I didn't know that living conditions could have been better. Even the harsh realities of being poor, coping with the severe and inclement winters, and the physically hard work that was always required to survive, did not lessen my enthusiasm for being alive. But many years later I realized that as a result of my boyhood upbringing and environment, I had been endowed with many characteristics that were to serve me well in future life. These included important traits like honesty, hard work, perseverance, self reliance, and love for family.

The following are fleeting recollections of mine about life in Westwood during those times. I can't describe each one of these in detail because it would be a huge task; but the reader should be assured that each recollection is a mini-story in itself.

Friends, neighbors, school chums, novelty of seeing touring cars with rumble seats and running boards, wild animals, picnics involving many Mexican families and including delicious food, baseball games, tug-of-wars, and races; lines at distribution centers for free food and coupons to get shoes, Christmas time, Thanksgiving Day when mother would invite the Guzmans from Old Town to share in our dinner (they were poorer than us if you can picture this), Fourth of July celebrations, church services, trips to recreation areas such as Lake Almanor and Eagle Lake.

School, wooden sidewalks, horse drawn milk wagon, lumber mill, mill pond, hauling small logs and tree branches on wagon from forest to our house, sawing and chopping wood, stacking cut wood in woodshed during summer for use in winter, snow everywhere in winter, icicles, cold outhouse in winter and stinky outhouse in summer, struggling to remove boulders from yard to build a rock fence, and growing a multitude of vegetables in our garden.

Raising chickens and rabbits, trapping squirrels in the woods, fishing, rafting and swimming in Robbers Creek, tree house, hospital, short pants, sling shots, games such as marbles, spinning tops, horseshoes, stilts, kites, and sleds; dirt roads and mud, railroad freight cars, Hoover Town (where hoboes hung out), bums asking mother for food (she made them do work before giving them any), Sears Roebuck catalog, girls, bloomers on girl's basketball team, carnivals that came into town, pot bellied stove, frozen water pipes, melting snow for water, and taking baths in a "tina" (metal round tub) too small for my body.

Winter clothes such as goggles, helmuts, ear muffs, mittens, and boots; rag balls to play catch with (the ball sure curved), Quaker Oats box used as a football, sisters' girl and boy friends, Saturday movies at the local theatre (admission cost was a nickel), delicious smells of mother's cooking of tortillas, cookies, and Mexican specialties; and 100 pound sacks of beans, rice and flour.

MY MOTHER, SIMONA REMARRIES

I realize now that part of the reason that my early boyhood growing years were enjoyable, was that my mother, Simona, shielded me from the raw elements of life. I thought life was O.K.; I didn't know any better. But for my mother, life in the early 1930's was still quite hard. Keeping the family together and coping with the harsh realities of our poor economic condition I'm sure played heavily on her mind. Even her best efforts to make ends meet did not seem to be enough. She reasoned that additional help was needed if her young family was to survive The Great Depression. So her dilemma was "what to do?"

Being a young widow in a small community, several men in town tried to obtain my mother's attention. One man named Jesus Ventura eventually asked Simona to marry him and after a lot of consideration, she agreed. It is my thought that this came about not because of love and affection, but because of self-sacrifice for the good of her young family; Ventura was employed part time and could help support her family in return for marital companionship. Simona insisted on marrying in the Church, and this was done in April, 1933. By July, 1933, Simona was pregnant once again, and on April 18, 1934 a baby girl named Amalia Josefina Ventura was born in Westwood hospital. Church records show that Amalia was baptized into the Catholic faith on September 15, 1934 by Father Joseph Cunha; the sponsors were Ignacio and Carmen Fernandez.

My recollections of Jesus Ventura were not very pleasant. He moved into the house on Robbers Creek with us and his presence was one of constant antagonism toward the children. He used profane language that had not been heard in our house previously, and no one could please him. So I, Ray, Tonia, and Janie just tried to ignore him. My mother was constantly protecting us against his tirades and abusive behavior and for her efforts he beat her. For the first time our home was not a happy one.

SISTER AT COLLEGE

Janie graduated from Westwood High in June, 1934. She wanted to help the family by staying in Westwood and getting a job. But my mother would not hear of this. Mother had been saving up money to pay for her daughter's college expenses for a long time. So that September my mother sent Janie away to college, thus fulfilling a long time dream she had for her oldest daughter. Janie went to the University of California at Berkeley to take business related courses. One must realize that sending Janie away to college was another sacrifice for my mother. Besides the expense involved, it meant that Janie could not get a job now to help support the rest of the children. Additionally, since Simona was now married, this meant that her plans for moving back to El Paso with her family had to be scrapped. One can only marvel at the resiliency of this woman as she struggled to do the best for her family!

By 1935, I was eleven years old and in the fifth grade at school. Physically I tended to be thin, but I was healthy and had good coordination skills. I was active in sports at school such as touch football, baseball, and track. I had my good share of school and neighborhood chums, even though I got into occasional fights with town bullies. I was a Tenderfoot Boy Scout, and my best school subjects were English and World History. At home we talked in Spanish because my mother brought us up that way. She preferred to talk in Spanish, however she could understand and say a few words in English.

THE HOT TAMALE CAPER

With Janie away at the university, the main burden of helping my mother around the house fell on Antonia, my older sister. She was in high school, but after school and on weekends, Tonia (as we called her), was constantly washing clothes, helping prepare the meals, working outside in the vegetable garden, or feeding the chickens. Tonia also had a key role in the family "tamale" endeavor, although Ray and I were also deeply involved.

Every Saturday for about a year, we made and sold hot tamales to supplement our family income. My mother and Tonia cooked the maize (corn) and meat in the mornings. Then Ray and I would take turns grinding the nixtamal (cooked corn) into the masa (dough). This was very hard work as the molino (grinder) was hand cranked. The masa was then mixed with other ingredients and the cooked meat was mixed with red chili sauce. After the spreading of the masa and meat onto the corn husks, the tamales were placed into large cylindrical cans and cooked on the wood stove. This took several hours and by late afternoon one could tell, by the pungent smells in the kitchen, that the tamales were cooked and ready for eating.

Next came the part I learned to hate; Ray and I now had to go all over town trying to sell those darn tamales. So off we went. We each had a pail full of hot tamales covered by a cloth to keep them warm. We knocked on doors in the neighborhood and after a few times we didn't have to make a sales pitch because everyone knew what we wanted. The price was 50 cents a dozen, but rarely did people buy a dozen; no one was flush with money. Usually they only bought a few at a nickel each. By all accounts these tamales tasted quite good and were considered a delicacy, as my mother was an expert tamale maker. The English speaking customers (gringos) especially raved over them.

If we sold a pail of tamales, we would then go back to the house for refills. Some days we sold our complete stock of tamales, but most of the time we didn't. If we had a good sales day, we were rewarded by going to the movies and by selecting one candy bar from my mother's candy stock. I might add that on bad selling days we were stuck with eating tamales for the remainder of the week. This doesn't sound all bad, but believe me after a while one gets tired of eating tamales, no matter how good.

MOTHER'S DEATH

During the early part of 1936, an event took place that changed my entire life. Simona, my mother, took sick with chronic pulmonary problems and was admitted to Westwood hospital on February 29, 1936. Dr. Fred J. Davis Sr. attended to her but at 7:15 p.m. on March 3, 1936, my mother passed away from this earth. The death certificate indicated the cause of death as double lobar pneumonia. She was only 38 years of age.

After all her trials and tribulations, this courageous and fine woman went to her reward in heaven. I shall always remember her as a true mother who was fun loving and full of life, who never complained, and one who deeply loved and cared for her children. She is buried in Lassen Cemetery, Susanville, California, Grave A, Lot 226, Section G. The gravestone is a marble piece with the following inscriptions: (top) Mother; (front) Rest in Peace, Recuerdo de Sposo y Hijos, Simona Ventura, March 25, 1900, March 3, 1936, At Rest.

> (It should be noted that according to my research the correct birth year should be 1897, not 1900).

The Herreras were now orphans. At the time of my mother's death our ages were as follows: Janie 20, Tonia 17, Jess 12, Raymond 10, Isobel 4, and Amalia Ventura was almost 2. A lot of things happened next. Quica Ramirez, my grandmother, had come to Westwood from El Paso as soon as she heard that my mother was gravely ill. So after Simona's death, Quica and Janie decided that the family should go to El Paso to live. The plan was as follows: Isobel and I were to go immediately to El Paso with my grandmother. After Tonia graduated from high school in June (3 months hence), the rest of the family would go to El Paso also. During this time Janie was to reach some accommodation with Jesus Ventura regarding disposition of the house on Robbers Creek. (Ventura stayed in Westwood although in the following years he made occasional visits to El Paso to see his daughter, Amalia).

I missed my beloved mother a lot and grieved for her. Words cannot express how bad I felt. Several weeks later the full impact of my loss hit me. I felt quite alone and sad because now I was without both a father and a mother. That fateful month of March, 1936 changed my entire life as I was now an orphan. However, I realized that my father, Albino, and my mother, Simona, had done all they could for me. Also, I knew that the Lord would provide all the support I needed in the future; all I had to do was to ask Him and trust in Him.

GOODBYE TO WESTWOOD

According to the plan, I left Westwood on March 15, 1936 along with my grandmother, Quica, and younger sister, Isobel. That trip to El Paso was quite a trek. We took a bus from Westwood to Sacramento. Then we took a four day train trip down the California Central Valley to Los Angeles, across the Arizona and New Mexico deserts, and on to El Paso. It was a my first ride ever on a bus or on a train; can you believe it? We made quite a trio and I'll never forget that trip. Quica was 70 years old at the time and knew no English. Isobel was practically still a baby and needed a lot of attention as she fussed a lot. We slept on the train or on the railstation benches awaiting our connections. The food we ate was all pre-prepared in Westwood; after a while it didn't taste so good in those hot stuffy train coach cars.

Additionally, I was not prepared for the responsibility of making sure we got to El Paso, but it turned out that it was up to me to make sure we did. My grandmother had travelled by train before, but I was the one that checked train schedules and communicated with agents, conductors and porters. This was especially tough when one remembers that worldly experiences for a 12 year old boy from a small lumber town, were quite limited. But with God's help we made it to El Paso, arriving on March 20, 1936. What the future held for me there, only He knew.

The one thing I knew was that my Westwood days were over.

4
Teen Years

FIRST TWO MONTHS IN EL PASO, TEXAS

Upon arrival in El Paso, Texas in late March, 1936, we immediately went to my grandmother's house at 803 South St. Vrain Street. This house was a small adobe cottage with stucco facing. The house contained a kitchen, living room, one bedroom, and an enclosed porch that served as an additional bedroom; it also had an indoor bathroom with a tub and toilet. The house was on a large lot adjoining some railroad tracks and there was yard space at the front, both sides, and at back. A woodshed adjoined the main house, and a small one room wooden structure was at the rear of the lot. With our arrival, there were four persons living in the main house, counting an uncle, Manuel, who also lived there.

One of the first things I did was to meet my uncle

and aunt, Luis and Maria Flores, and my cousins. The Flores were a large family consisting of eight boys and one girl. This family lived a few blocks from my grandmother's house, very near the U.S.- Mexico border. One of the boys, Jose, was about my age and we immediately struck up a friendship that exists to this day. Joe, as I called him, was not only a good playmate but he in effect took me under his wing and by his example taught me a lot about life and survival in a "big" city.

Joe Flores was enrolled in the sixth grade at Alamo Elementary Public School, and with his help I also was placed into that class to finish out the school year. I was not sure how I would do in this new school environment because it was quite difficult for me to adapt to a very different culture. The school was in South El Paso, which meant the Mexican "barrios". The lifestyle here was a lot different from what I had been exposed to in Westwood. At first I did not get along very well with my classmates because I was the new kid on the block and was naive about a lot of things.

Also, everyone talked Spanish mostly, and a type of slang which I had never heard before. Since I could talk English without a Mexican accent, this made me different and so I was not very popular. Compared to others I excelled in my English and Speech classes. The teachers, who were all Anglo, did not help the acceptance situation any, because they held me up before my classmates as an example of how to talk "properly". The class bullies picked many a fight with me at recess time during those months, and Joe Flores had to come to my aid more than once. Nevertheless, I survived, and in June I was promoted into the seventh grade and was to transfer to Aoy Junior High School commencing that next September. I was glad when vacation time arrived because those first two months in El Paso had not been much fun for me.

SUMMER AND FALL, 1936

I soon found out during those first few months, that the summer weather in El Paso was not pleasant. The temperature was always around 100 degrees, and the air was either deadly still or else a hot dusty wind blew sand and grime everywhere. During the day, it was impossible to stay indoors because of the sun's heat, and at night one was bathed in sweat because it didn't cool off much. Bugs of all types were everywhere. Somehow people got used to this hot dry climate but the pace of living was slow.

That summer in 1936 there wasn't much for me to do, so I decided to read a lot. Books just fascinated me. I made daily trips to the public library in the mornings and brought home three or four books which I read in the afternoon in the shade by the side of the house. The books were of all kinds; sports, adventure, Indian and frontier, travel, history, fiction and non-fiction. Stories about The Knights of the Round Table and biographies of sports immortals like Red Grange and Babe Ruth were impressionable tales for me.

Additionally, I helped my ageing grandmother around the house, taking care of the yards, and running errands to the grocery store for her. I remember my grandmother sending me to buy a dime's worth of "carne molida" for the evening meal; but I soon found out that one pound of this meat cost nine cents, so I always bought one pound and used the other penny for a cookie or candy for myself. The butcher, "Pancho", always carefully weighed one pound of meat and then with a sly look would ask me what else I wanted. By the time I made it back to the house I was in good spirits.

Another episode that I remember quite vividly was how I used to help my grandmother make homemade beer. I used to ladle the homebrew from the vats into bottles; I would then cap the bottles and store them away. Of course, I wasn't allowed to taste the stuff but Quica my grandmother sampled the beer to see if it was o.k.; it must have been potent stuff because Quica would soon wind up crying and reminiscing about her long lost sons. I just stood around perplexed as to what was going on.

The rest of the Herrera family arrived from Westwood in July, 1936 and settled in at my grandmother's house. However, with eight persons now crammed into this small house, it was soon obvious that we could not stay there long because of the crowded conditions. Fortunately, Janie soon got a job at the American Furniture Store in downtown El Paso as a bookkeeper/stenographer. She then looked for another place where we could live. She rented one half of an upstairs flat at 504 South Park Street and that Fall we moved there. The upstairs flat had a an outdoor front porch at the front of the house and had a long central hall from front to back. The owner, Josefina Quintanar, her husband and three kids, lived on one side of the hallway. We occupied the other side across the hallway. Our new home consisted of a miniscule kitchen, and two small bedrooms. A common bathroom was shared with the Quintanar family. So Janie, Tonia, Ray and I, and Isobel lived in this flat for the ensuing years. Because of lack of space, and because my grandmother apparently had more time to take care of a two year old, Amalia Ventura, my other sister, continued to live with my grandmother at her house.

That fall I attended Aoy Junior High, which was a public school in South El Paso. By this time I was more socially accepted by my classmates as "one of them", and so I got along better. I did well in my studies at this school, as by now I was in the right sequence of classes and only a couple of the teachers were very demanding in their assignments. I realized much later that the formal education one receives in the "barrios" was not of rigorous quality. So at the completion of one school year, I graduated from Aoy Junior High School in El Paso in June, 1937 and was then ready to enter a new phase of my life's education at Bowie High School. I was 13 years old.

THE CORNER

During the 1937 summer vacation, boredom set in so I turned to books once again. I continued my voracious reading of any books I could get my hands on; daily trips to the public library was a form of diversion for me. Also once in the vicinity of the library, which was downtown, I could occupy myself by looking at the department store windows and scanning through the magazines at the newsstands. I didn't have many chores at home except to feed Isobel, replenish the ice in the ice box and throw away the melted icewater, and make up my bed; this was nothing compared to all the work I previously had to do in Westwood. I went to visit Joe Flores as often as I could but his time was regimented because his parents were quite strict and he had to help around the house most of the time. The rest of the time I spent just hanging around the street corner from where we lived.

This corner at South Park and 3rd Street was right opposite San Ignacio Catholic Church and was the gathering place for all the neighborhood kids; young and old, good and bad. This corner was a beehive of activity and we spent hours there, day and night. All the kids, myself included, played cards (Casino), pitched pennies, shot dice, played a form of handball called "rebote" against the building walls, played makeshift football, baseball, and basketball, read comic books, and just plain loafed.

Sundays were a big day for the denizens of this street corner because we could watch all the people going to and from Sunday mass at the church. Also the spectacle of everyone dressed in their Sunday best clothes, or that of a wedding party or of a baptism party on the church steps, certainly broke up the monotony of our daily lives. Occasionally, arguments flared up among the kids at the "corner"; but by and large it was just a place where they congregated to get away from the oppressive tenement slum houses (red brick buildings called "presidios") where they lived, and to socialize. Of course everyone in the neighborhood was a Mexican-American (Chicano), and by any standards everyone was quite poor. Another memory I have is that everyone had a nickname; some of them were funny, but most of them were descriptive like "el Gordo" or "el Flacco". In the neighborhood I was given the nickname "Califa Grande" (because I came from California), and Raymond my brother, was "Califa Chico".

HAPPY TIMES

That Fall in 1937, I started at Bowie High School. At that time in El Paso, there were only three district high schools and students had to attend the high school in the district where they lived. For those of us who lived in the 2nd Ward, Bowie was the place. The school itself was located in South El Paso near the U. S. - Mexico border. I enjoyed my four years at Bowie High School and I still consider this period as one of the most memorable times of my life. My classmates were by now all good friends and since I was in the teen years of my life I was at an impressionable age. I started to notice girls in a different light for the first time but was chagrined to find out that I was a "novice" at even striking up a conversation with one. However, with coaching from the more adventuresome boys, I soon became comfortable in talking to girls in my class, and thereafter got along well with them.

In the late 1930's and early 1940's one of the things that made this a "happy" period, and certainly helped the girl situation, was the advent of the big band era. It was during this time that the nationwide popularity of this form of music was at it's peak. The "swing" and ballad hits of the day were played constantly on the radio and juke boxes, and a big band phonograph record collection (78 rpm recordings) was a personal goal of every teenager. The big band hits recorded on 78's were played over and over again; everyone memorized the choruses and instrument solos.

Big time swing bands like Tommy Dorsey, Benny Goodman, Charlie Barnett, Artie Shaw, Count Basie, Glenn Miller, Jimmie Lunceford, Duke Ellington, and countless of others, were the rage of the day. What music! To this day I thoroughly enjoy listening to the full sound of the sax and brass sections, as exemplified by the big bands of the 1930's and 1940's. As it turned out, my love for this kind of music led to my learning to play an instrument; but I'm getting ahead of my story.

Dancing and listening to this type of music became the accepted social way to have fun, and also to mingle with girls. Fortunately for me, Janie and Tonia taught me how to dance and I practiced at home with them. At school, afternoon tea dances to the tunes on "78" records were held every week, and of course night dances and proms were held, with live bands on special occasions. Also, numerous house parties at the slightest pretext, helped to make this a fun time in my life.

INFLUENCE OF JESUIT PRIEST

It was during the summer of 1938, that Padre Acosta, a Spanish Jesuit priest at San Ignacio Catholic Church, had a big influence on my development as a youth. Apparently this priest was saddened to see us kids wasting our time just hanging around in the corner across from his church. So somehow in his neighborhood ministry, this priest cajoled and talked a few of us "barrio" ruffians into participating in his activities.

The deal was that if we agreed to become altar boys, and take Latin, catechism, and music classes from him, then he in turn would allow us to play in his fenced-in churchyard; and furthermore he would provide all the kickballs, tennis balls, soccer balls, basketballs, tetherballs,and footballs that we needed to play with. What luxury we thought, to play with real sports equipment; all we had to do was to go through the motions in his classes. Little did we know that this little fat priest was serious about trying to instill some Godly faith and discipline into our lives!

Suffice to say that I was an altar boy at San Ignacio Catholic Church for the next three years. I served at daily and Sunday masses at all hours of the day, as well as at special functions like funerals, weddings, baptisms, processions, and at church holy days and church feast days like Christmas and Easter. The responses at holy mass were all in Latin, so I have to admit that the Latin classes were necessary; even though in most cases I didn't know what the Latin words actually meant.

We were also required to attend his catechism classes that he held for public school kids. I can't say that I absorbed very much as a result of these sessions, but he drilled us constantly on the teachings of the Catholic Church.

What I really hated was the music reading lessons. There were no instruments; all we did was to sing church hymms aloud by reading the notes on sheet music. This was all done in a hot stuffy church basement whose temperature was humanly intolerable. We did this for an hour every day for one complete summer. I can still picture this priest with his face and Roman collar bathed in perspiration, in a black cassock, with his arms waving and marking time for a few young Chicanos who at that moment were probably thinking ahead of playing in the schoolyard or of girls.

In Spanish this exercise was called "solfeo", i.e. the art of reading notes from a music book and then singing the tunes, but without any instrument accompaniment. At the time I didn't think I was learning anything of any earthly value, but grudgingly I had to admit that I did learn to read music that Summer. However, little did I know that by the dedication of this man of faith he was being God's instrument in my development as an individual. As it turned out, I owe a lot to Padre Acosta, who by now has obtained his just reward in heaven.

LIFE AT BOWIE HIGH

Student life at Bowie High was exciting and interesting; I enjoyed going to school. The complete student body was made up of Mexican-Americans; there were no blacks (they went to Douglas school which was segregated and only for blacks), and the only Anglo at Bowie was a girl who was the daughter of the school janitor. There were no college prep courses. All the boys took a trades curriculum, like woodworking and welding, and the girls took a commercial course, like typing, shorthand and homemaking. Of course everyone took history, english, and basic math courses.

The sports program at Bowie was a vibrant one. Football, track and basketball were the main competitive sports but basketball was the only sport that we were any good at. I still remember the local newspaper sports pages proclaim "EZ BOYS WIN (or LOSE) AGAIN." The reason for this was that most everybody's name on the team ended in "ez"; i.e. names like Ramirez, Melendez, Fernandez, Gomez, Alvarez, etc. At Bowie I participated only in intramural sports, and I belonged to various clubs (speech, debating, National Honor Society, etc.) and the school band.

I joined the Bowie High School band in the fall term of 1939 because Joe Flores, who was already in the band, talked me into trying out. As a new member, I got to use only the leftover instruments; i.e. instruments that no one else wanted. So I started out on the C-Melody saxophone, which was an ungainly instrument. My musical progress was fairly rapid, or so I thought, since I could read music. Nevertheless, playing complicated marches and trying to catch the nuances of symphonic scores was a far cry from what I knew. However, the band director Mr. Esterly, needed us newcomers in the band in order to fill out the ranks. The band spent long hours at rehearsals and as a result the band was actually very good. During marching competitions however, the director didn't want us newcomers to play any sour notes so he advised us to just keep in step and hold the instrument up to our lips. But he didn't want us to play any notes. It was obvious that he had no confidence in us.

As it turned out, several key band members graduated in June 1940, and so that summer out of necessity to replenish the ranks, Mr. Esterly asked me and three others, to take some advanced music lessons from him. So three times a week I went to the music store where Mr. Esterly worked during the summer, and took private lessons. I was in heaven during those sessions because I could use the store's brand new gold plated instruments to practice on, and also had all the reeds that I needed. I could not take the saxophone home however, so at home I practiced the assigned lessons by fingering the notes on a rolled up magazine and at the same time singing out the notes. By the end of the summer, I had progressed musically far beyond my expectations.

When school started that Fall I was amazed to find that I could play songs and scores that previously had seemed like Greek to me. I was rewarded by being assigned to play the First Chair in the saxophone section. My instrument was Eb alto saxophone and for the ensuing year I continued to practice and develop my skills as a musician. I probably drove the neighborhood crazy by playing the sax every spare moment I had. I'm sure the music was not too pleasant for others to hear since my practice consisted mostly of fingering exercises, scales, and etudes. But no one complained too loudly, so I continued to toot my horn.

HIGH SCHOOL TEACHERS

The teachers at Bowie High, with one or two exceptions, were all Anglo and mostly females except for the athletic coaches and the shop and ROTC instructors. My recollection of the teachers is one of admiration for their dedication to us students. I know that their concern for us poor unfortunate "barrio" kids was genuine. They tried their best to educate us and to instill in us the values of being good citizens, even though they could see the tremendous odds that any one of us faced, what with poverty, lack of opportunity, and racial discrimination all around us. I think besides the student life, another reason why my Bowie High School days were so memorable and happy was that the teachers treated everyone with respect. Furthermore, they were loyal and they helped us in every way they could. I personally got along very well with several of the teachers. As I scan through the pages of teachers in my 1941 yearbook, "THE AZTEC", my mind flashes to their presence in school plays, civic classes, R.O.T.C., term papers, final exams, exhortations to talk in English (not Spanish) in class, and general guidance.

Furthermore, I remember quite vividly teacher incidents like when the band was competing in district competition at Big Springs, Texas. At first we were not allowed to sleep in the town hotel nor eat in the town cafe (we were asked to go eat in the kitchen). The local citizenry did not take kindly to Mexican-Americans. Our Anglo teacher chaperones were outraged at this and threatened to pull the band out of the competition if we were not treated more humanely. Since we were representing all the schools of El Paso, the promoters eventually intervened and we got something to eat, and a place to sleep that night.

On a personal note I also remember Miss Bivens, an English teacher, taking me on an after school job hunting tour in downtown El Paso. We went up and down every street, and into every retail store, seeking a job for me. I was 16 at the time and finally with this teacher's help I got my first-ever job at the Popular Dry Goods Department Store as a "cash boy" at ten cents an hour. This was not much pay, but at least it gave me some spending money. I worked daily after school and on most Saturdays.

HIGH SCHOOL GRADUATION

The highlight of my last two years at Bowie was attending the Junior and Senior proms. My date both times was a belle named Concha Cadena. She was a year or two older than I and not exactly my girlfriend; she was just one of the gang of friends that I knew. However the proms were a lot of fun and were the social highlight of the schoolyear. The proms were gala affairs held in the school auditorium and we had the best orchestra in town. The girls were all decked out in long formal evening gowns and the guys all had rented tuxedos. I wore a white jacket with black pants and a red bow tie.

I graduated from Bowie High School on June 1, 1941 at the age of 17. Out of a class of 75, I had the third highest four year grade average.

So as my teen years were coming to an end, I realized that I had just gone through a very memorable growing up period of my life. I thought I had learned a lot in the last four to five years and was proud of myself for graduating from high school. Little did I know that all I had done was to reach another plateau in my life.

5
College Years

LIFE AFTER HIGH SCHOOL

The days and months immediately following graduation from high school were lonely times and a big letdown from the excitement of being a senior at Bowie. I did not have any plans for the future; except possibly to find a job. I did not see my friends from school any longer on a regular basis, and so I just kind of drifted not knowing nor caring about the future.

I found work as a stock boy in the piece goods department of Lerners on Stanton Street in El Paso. The owner was a big Jewish man named Herskowitz. My job as to unpack the bolts of material and set them out on the store tables in a neat configuration. I also helped affix the price tags onto the merchandise, and also ran errands as requested. The pay was $8.00 a week for a six day work week. It was a boring job because there wasn't much to do. The only times we were real busy was during a sale. Then pandemonium would set in. The ladies would swoop onto my neatly arranged bolts of cloth, unroll them, look at them, then cast the material aside in a crumpled heap. They would then go on to the next roll of material or table and do the same thing until the whole place was in a state of disarray. Piles of unfurled and unfolded material were all over the place. I could not keep the place neat because the ladies did not cooperate, but the boss didn't seem to mind because merchandise was being sold.

Another memory I have about this job was that on Saturday nights when the store was open late, Mr. Herskowitz would give me a quarter (25 cents) for dinner. For my meal, I would go to adjacent stores and get a hot dog for a dime, and a coke and a Baby Ruth candy bar for a nickel each. This left me with an extra nickel which made me feel that I was outwitting the boss.

During those times, wages for workers were not very high, especially in El Paso where unions had not gained a stronghold. On the other hand the price for services and for goods were not very high either; one could get a pair of tennis shoes for under $2.00, a haircut for 15 to 25 cents, a complete dinner (called a "plate lunch") at a cafe for less than 50 cents, and go to the movies for between 15 and 35 cents. By the way, one got his money's worth at the movies; there were usually two main features, a comedy short, a newsreel, and a "chapter" of a serial adventure or western saga. Additionally there were film clips of the coming attractions.

To keep busy at nights and on weekends, brother

Ray and I played baseball at Armijo Park or at the "llano" (an open field). We joined a team that played in both softball and hardball leagues. I was a pitcher and I learned how to throw curve balls from books. These activities were fun and the games were well attended (free) by spectators. Sometimes however not all our players showed up for a game. Also, the playing field at the "llano" was full of rocks and high weeds. So if anybody could hit the ball beyond the infield there was a good chance that he could circle the bases while the fielders were looking for the ball amongst the weeds and gopher holes.

ORCHESTRA PLAYING DAYS

During the Summer of 1941, I tried to keep up with my music playing. By this time my main interest was in playing dance music. I bought an alto saxophone and attempted to form an orchestra. I recruited four other guys that I knew from my school days and we started to practice. However, none of these players were very good musicians; nor could they "ad lib" any songs or solos. Since we could not immediately afford any sheet music we were in trouble from the start. Nevertheless, I reasoned that if we could get a couple of playing dates under our belts we could use our fee money to buy sheet music. So I composed two songs and wrote out the music parts for the trumpet, alto sax, and tenor sax. I also specified the chords for the piano, but the drummer was on his own; his job was to keep the beat. We practiced my two original swing songs and I set out to find someone who would hire us.

Our first engagement was for a coming out party for a debutant in one of the classier sections of North El Paso. We started off with an entrance march that I made up on the spot. All the formally attired guests filed into the room.

We then played the first of our two songs and the kids danced and had fun. We followed this with our next tune and everyone clapped when the song was over. But then disaster struck! After we had repeated these two tunes of mine over and over, the folks started to get restless and inquired if we could play something else. Needless to say we couldn't, and from that point on the party was essentially over. However we did get paid.

Our next dance gig was at a baptism house party in my own neighborhood. This event was quite informal but again we ran into trouble. We started off by playing my two original songs, but the people soon tired of these and so they asked us to play Mexican folk and traditional songs. We tried to play this kind of music, but at times I was the only one playing, since my companions just couldn't play any of these songs. To add to our troubles, the piano at that house was woefully out of tune and we could not tune the remainder of the instruments properly, so we must have sounded bad.

I decided that this orchestra of mine was going nowhere, so I disbanded it shortly after.

One good thing that came out of this ill fated venture was that soon thereafter, a local orchestra called the "Swing Kings" needed a sax player. They asked me to try out with them, and so I did. This orchestra played for all types of occasions, formal and informal, in El Paso, as well as in surrounding communities in Texas and in New Mexico. I played with this orchestra for the next two years and as time went on, my dance band musicianship improved. The musicians in this band were all Mexican-Americans except for the piano player who was a Negro. Every member was an excellent musician; they knew hundreds of songs by "heart", and also had an excellent book of popular big band dance hits. I learned and honed my skills as a musician with this group. However character wise I wouldn't say they were a very good example. They drank a lot, and even though they were all married, caroused frequently with women after the dance dates and in Juarez, Mexico.

I did enjoy this time of my life however. Every one seemed to be having fun. The dance craze and "big band" era was still in full swing. This was the time of the zoot suit, jitterbugging, juke boxes, and romantic ballads. Several big name orchestras came to the El Paso Liberty Hall to play for dances. Upon recalling this, I remember that the South, including Texas, was segregated. Negro (Black) folks had to use separate facilities from the white folks. This included schools, movie houses and other public establishments. For example, in El Paso the department stores had two side by side drinking fountains; one was labelled "whites", and the other had a sign which read "colored". Furthermore, the black people had to ride in the rear of the city busses in a special section reserved for them; the white folks of course rode in the front sections.

So as a result of this segregation, whenever a white orchestra like Tommy Dorsey's came to Liberty Hall, all the white folks danced on the main floor and the black folks just listened to the music from the balcony. Then when a black band like Count Basie's came to town, the roles were reversed and the black folks danced and the white people were in the balcony.

At the time, these various forms of discrimination against the black folks stirred my conscience, and I felt sorry for them. However, I was more aware of the overt forms of job, education, and social discrimination in El Paso and the Southwest against Mexican-Americans. This was real for me. What bothered me about this was that I knew that the Mexican-American people had contributed greatly to the culture of the Southwestern part of our country. Our people had a proud heritage and they had continued to build on their strengths of tradition, good character, strong values, family, and Catholic religion. Yet, discrimination abounded. Nevertheless, Mexican- Americans kept their spirits up and tried to enjoy life.

The various social clubs of the Mexican-American community in El Paso sponsored many public dances in various halls and environs. The most popular locations were the ballrooms of the three main hotels in El Paso, i.e. The Cortez, The Hilton, and The Paso Del Norte. The dances there were mostly formal evening affairs, although some late afternoon tea dances or "tardeadas" were also held. The Swing Kings orchestra was one of the two best and most popular local bands and so we were in high demand. We played someplace every weekend but the formality and the grandeur of the hotel dances were my favorite dance jobs. I can still picture the Chicano guys and gals all dressed in formal evening wear, dancing away the night.

As an aside, I might mention that I usually had a date with a girl on these dance nights. However, all this meant was that I escorted my date to and from the dance; since I was busy playing in the band I couldn't dance with anyone. I might add that my dates always seemed to have a lot of fun; i.e. they just didn't hang around the bandstand watching me play - they weren't that loyal! However, I didn't mind; I still considered them my girlfriends. Life was simple and even though we still lived in the barrios, somehow the magic of the music of the 1940's took our minds away from the harsh realities of our everyday existence. That period of my life was one of full enjoyment and growing into manhood.

THE BEGINNING OF WORLD WAR 2

On December 7, 1941 an event happened that changed the life of millions of people all over the world. The Japanese bombed the U.S. naval base at Pearl Harbor in Hawaii. On December 8th, President Franklin Delano Roosevelt and the U. S. Congress declared war on Japan. Three days later, this was followed with a declaration of war against the German-Italian axis led by Hitler and Mussolini. Life across the U.S. and in El Paso was changed dramatically and immediately.

The Selective Training and Service Act (The Draft) was instituted in which all male citizens ages 18 through 44 were ordered to register with their draft boards for possible induction into the armed services of the country. And so as early as the Spring of 1942 several of my friends either joined the services or were inducted into the Army and Navy. I, of course, registered with the draft board and fully expected to be called up to take my physical examination.

In the meantime however, I had changed jobs and was now working as a carpenter's helper at the Southern Pacific maintentance facility in El Paso. This job required heavy manual labor and involved hammering, sawing, and hauling lumber for the building of small houses for the railroad section crews. At the end of every day I was so tired that I could hardly drag myself home. My wages had improved however, and I was now making $1.00 an hour; which at least left some money for me after helping Janie and Toni with the house expenses. However, I figured I was just marking time before going into the service. I was classified 1A, which meant single status, no dependents, and thus subject to call-up at any time.

What happened next was totally unexpected, and at the time the biggest disappointment of my life. Upon taking my physical examination prior to induction into the service, a battery of Army doctors did not pass me. They claimed that I had a marginal heart murmur (leaky heart valve) that prevented me from being immediately inducted into the service. So I was classified temporarily as 4F; meaning not fit for active duty. I was to be reexamined again in six months. I was devastated at this turn of events! I had always been in good health and I couldn't accept the doctors' findings. During those times, it was unpatriotic to not be in the service, and my youthful inner feelings left me hurt and sad, because mentally I had prepared myself to go into the armed services.

I had long assumed that Mexican-Americans would forever be destined to just exist; without any hope for a better life outside the "barrios". That had been my experience to date. So one of my reasons for wanting to go into the service was that I could see an opportunity to change my life. The service had an adventuresome ring to it; I never thought about the danger involved. Most of the people I knew were drafted into the army as Privates with no particular skills, nor did they have any apparent motivation to advance. But when one of my high school friends who joined the Air Force took an examination and was admitted into Officers Candidate School, I realized that Chicanos from the ghetto had just as much intelligence and potential as anyone else. This realization stimulated my mind and unleashed every fiber within me. When this friend later got his 2nd Lieutenant's Wings as a pilot in the Air

Force I was so proud. This buddy never knew it, but he greatly influenced my thinking about life. A sad note however; this classmate of mine, years later, was killed in combat in Europe.

MY EARLY COLLEGE YEARS

Up to this time in my life, it had never entered my mind, even for a fleeting moment, to go to college. But to shake me out of my lethargy and disappointment at not being in the service, my sisters Janie and Tonia encouraged me to further my education. An accepted way to avoid being immediately drafted into the armed services in the 1940's was to obtain a college student deferment. Jose Flores, my cousin, and a couple of other high school friends who had college deferments, were enrolled at Texas College of Mines in El Paso and so I decided to do the same. Fortunately, I had a little money saved up from working for the past year. So in September, 1942, I started at Texas College of Mines taking a general engineering curriculum.

During this time, Raymond my brother, who had graduated from Bowie high School in June 1942, was just marking time before being inducted into the armed services. Tonia and Juanita were working, and Isobel was still in grade school. So our family was still intact and we continued to lived on Park Street in El Paso. However, as it turned out, I was now embarking on a new phase of my life. I prayed that God would be with me.

Once again nothing came easy for me. It was soon apparent that my Bowie High School education had not adequately prepared me to take college level courses. I was especially deficient in mathematics and in science, including physics and chemistry. The preparatory english, history, and other general education courses were O.K. however. So it turned out that I wound up taking many make up courses for no college credit during my early semesters. But I was determined to persevere in college and the professors and instructors at that school were helpful and encouraged me to continue. But I was always behind most other students in my classes, since I had so much catching up to do. It took great effort on my part to do college level work because the study and laboratory demands on my time were heavy. The requirements were a far cry from that which I was accustomed to in high school.

Texas College of Mines (later called Texas Western, and still later called University of Texas-El Paso), was an interesting school located in the Franklin Mountains in northeast El Paso. In the early 1940's the school offered four year degrees in Liberal Arts and in Mining/Metallurgical technology. The remainder of the curriculum served as a two year preparation for advanced Engineering and other Sciences at other universities. The small group of us Chicano collegians at this school did not participate in any of the campus social events because our demanding engineering courses took up most of our time. Generally we were not received very cordially by other students; but we didn't care.

An activity that I remember quite vividly while at this college was in my physical education class (P.E.). The college was having a boxing tournament and everyone taking P.E. had to participate. In 1943 I was a skinny guy weighing about 125 pounds and about 5'-9" tall. My boxing skills were not too bad but I didn't like this sport because even with large cushion-like 12 ounce gloves, the blows one received still hurt.

The problem was that I kept winning one bout after another, so as I advanced in the tournament I had to keep fighting. Each bout consisted of only three one minute rounds; but the fatigue and exhaustion between the rounds were unbelievable. Joe Flores was my "manager" and in between rounds he kept dousing me with water and shaking my arms and legs, and giving me advice. All I wanted was to slump in my corner and be left alone in my misery. I was dead tired.

Finally in the semi-finals of the championship, I lost my match by a split decision. I was elated; it was all over for me! But not quite, as it turned out. The guy that had beaten me took sick on the eve of the grand championship Sports Night and I was required to fill in for him. I went into this match with much trepidation because now we were to use eight ounce gloves. These gloves were very light and of course would hurt all the more. Well to make a long story shorter, the final bout turned out to be an easy one for me. There was no one more surprised than I, when I knocked my opponent to the canvas in the first round and the fight was stopped by the referee. I could have kissed the referee at that moment, not because I was the school champ of my weight class, but because I didn't have to box anymore!

For all my boxing efforts I was given a ring as a prize. I was proud of this ring but later, in my youthful exuberance, I lent it to a girlfriend whose name I don't even remember now. The ring was never returned to me. What a waste.

My course of study at Texas College of Mines continued straight through 1943, including Summer semesters, and into the Spring of 1944. By now my Draft registration was in a 3A student deferment basis. The Services evidently allowed young men to complete their college education so that afterwards they would be prime candidates for Officer training. In fact, all the universities in the country had servicemen on their campuses enrolled in college curriculums under special Army, Navy, or Air Force Programs. These men were in the Military but in effect going to school while World War 2 waged on.

It was soon time for me to transfer to another University to continue my engineering studies. Several of my close friends were transferring to a school now known as New Mexico State University in Las Cruces, which was only about 45 miles north of El Paso. I was thinking of doing the same but an instructor at Texas College of Mines strongly suggested that I consider going to Texas A&M University instead. He recommended this school as the best engineering school in the whole Southwest. So I applied there and was accepted in July, 1944.

YEARS AT TEXAS A&M UNIVERSITY; 1944-1946

By Fall 1944, Raymond my brother, had been inducted into the Air Force, and Isobel, my younger sister, had just started high school. Juanita and Tonia, my older sisters, had boy friends but had not married; principally because of the responsibility they felt towards us younger members of the family. Juanita and Tonia both encouraged me to continue my education and committed to help pay for college expenses. So even though I had some misgivings about being away from home for the first time in my life, I boarded a Greyhound bus in El Paso in September, 1944 and set out for the Agricultural & Mechanical College of Texas (Texas A&M).

Texas A&M is located in College Station, Texas which is in the Southeastern part of the state in Brazos County. Little did I realize that this school is almost 700 road miles distance from El Paso. So by the time the bus dropped me off, I was homesick already. There I was in the middle of the Texas plains, about to embark on a new educational effort, among total strangers and with no friends for support. I almost got back on the bus, but by this time it had taken off down the road.

The Texas A&M school grounds were very spacious and the campus was so large that a bus line ran through it. I was surprised to find out that the college was in effect an ROTC (Reserve Officers Training Corp) military school. This meant among other things that all students belonged to the Cadet Corp, they lived on campus in dormitories, and all wore uniforms; also every student was male, there were no women admitted at that time. All student life, outside the classrooms, was controlled by the student officers of the Cadet Corp.

Life on campus was very difficult for me, especially in the beginning. I just was not conditioned mentally to accept the discipline and regimentation that I was immediately exposed to. The school is one with very rich traditions in student and alumni loyalty, in sports, academics and research, and of course the military. Everyone has heard of the "Texas Aggies" all over the world. However, at first, I was quite unhappy because it was very hard for me to fit into the student campus life, in this my temporary new home. While I suffered no overt acts of discrimination by other students, there was certainly no welcome mat out for a Chicano from South El Paso. Even my roommates hardly ever talked to me.

The Lord helped me however. Just when my spirits were low, a man named Taylor Wilkins looked me up. This man was an officer in the regular army and was assigned to Texas A&M as an ROTC instructor. However, he had previously been assigned to work at Bowie High School in El Paso, where I had known him and developed a friendship. One cannot imagine my surprise and joy at seeing and talking with Lt. Wilkins! For the next two years in school, he was my confidant and was the one local person that gave me continual support and encouragement. Once again the Lord had sent some one to help me get over a tough hurdle in life.

Because of my initial difficulties in adjusting to student life at Texas A&M, I actually looked forward to time spent in the classrooms. Here of course there was only the discipline of instruction and of learning; no one could pull rank on you and acceptance by the professors depended solely on how well you did the assigned work. I had decided to major in Electrical Engineering. Since I was a transfer student, not all of my previous course work was accepted at Texas A&M for credit. Therefore academically, I only had a Sophomore standing. This meant that I wound up taking some lower division courses just to fulfill all the requirements. Once again this catching up on course work meant that for the next two years, I had to take heavy course loads every semester.

From the very beginning, the academic requirements at A&M were much more demanding than what I had experienced at Texas College of Mines. One could immediately tell why Texas A&M had such a fine academic reputation. The instructors were excellent and committed, and the classes were fairly small. The whole student body numbered only about 8000; this low enrollment was due of course to the ongoing World War 2. There was only a handful of Hispanics in the whole school and most of these were foreign students. I met most of these at Sunday Mass, which was held in a small off campus chapel. Today in 1991, the university has a huge enrollment of over 35,000, of which about 20% are from a racial or ethnic minority group. Additionally, the school has long been co-ed. The Corp of Cadets is still very active but is small compared to the total student population. How times have changed!

THE AGGIELAND ORCHESTRA

Probably the most memorable and enjoyable experience for me while at Texas A&M was my involvement in the Aggieland Orchestra. This was a school organization that played for dances and variety shows on campus at least two times a week. I auditioned and was selected as a member early in 1945. My previous El Paso experience as a musician of course served me well. The band was a large professionally run outfit of about 18 members, and with a director and our own arrangers and singers. I played the alto and tenor saxophones, as well as clarinet, with this orchestra. Since the A&M campus is literally in the middle of nowhere, the entertainment value of this orchestra was tremendous, and the students loved our performances. Girls from nearby colleges flocked to the campus to attend the dances; especially on football game weekends.

At times during weekends or holiday periods, the orchestra went on the road. We travelled by special bus to various towns and cities in Central and South Texas to play for dances sponsored by the various A&M Alumni clubs from those localities. We were a big hit and well received by everyone. We not only played the popular tunes of the day, but also played the various A&M traditional school and fight songs like, "The Spirit of Aggieland" and "The Aggie War Hymn". The enthusiasm and fun of all who attended these functions will forever be etched in my memory.

We were paid quite well for our orchestra services. I received from six to ten dollars an hour depending on the event. This in fact is what paid for most of my tuition, books, and room & board while at Texas A&M. The remainder of the expenses I received from my sisters and my brother. I received no other financial aid. Little did I know many years previous when Padre Acosta gave me music lessons, that he would be instrumental in my being able to finance my college education. This proves once again, that throughout life one needs only to trust in the Lord; He knows what's best for us.

FINAL YEAR AT TEXAS A&M

As time went on, I gradually came to enjoy my stay at Texas A&M. I matured fast in adapting to the demands of college life. I didn't get to go home very often during holidays or Spring break times, either because of the large distance and travel expense of going to El Paso, or because of my studies. When I did visit home I hitched hiked. During those visits to El Paso I was a popular guy with the girls; mostly, I now suspect, because there were not too many boys around. Every able bodied man was in the service. In fact one of my problems was that a couple of my hometown girl friends kept pushing me to marry them. The pressure was difficult for me, but somehow I was able to resist the temptations offered, as I was determined to finish my college education.

When I reached Senior standing, I was made a 1st Lieutenant in the Cadet Corp Battalion Staff. My uniform was changed to resplendant military garb including riding breeches and leather boots. I was proud of the boots because they cost me a small fortune. As a Senior, I acquired campus privileges which actually meant less regimentation in my student life. My classwork progressed well because by now I was taking electrical power system courses, which was my chosen field of specialization.

Finally, I successfully completed my course of study, and on May 31, 1946, I was awarded a Batchelor of Science Degree in Electrical Engineering from Texas A&M University. My sister Janie attended the graduation ceremonies at school and the next day we both returned to El Paso. I was very proud to be the first member of our family to obtain a four year college degree. Special thanks and appreciation goes to my sisters Janie and Tonia, and my brother Ray, for their support during my college years.

A very rewarding and confidence building part of my life was over. I will forever cherish the traditional and beautiful Texas A&M class ring that I now had on my finger. It represented a reward for a lot of hard work and sacrifice by myself and my family. It is my fervent wish that my descendants keep this ring in the family and look upon it as a symbol of committment to their education.

As I write these words many decades later, I believe that getting a college education was a very important event that changed the course of my life. It was the key to opening the door for me out of a mundane existence in the "barrios". My college education exposed my mind to vistas I never even dreamed about, and it resulted in a fuller life for me, my wife, and my children.

6
Courtship
and Marriage

WORLD WAR 2 ENDS

By June 1946, World War 2 was essentially over and many historical events had transpired while I was in college. The U.S. and Allied forces had begun the liberation of Europe and landed on the Normandy Coast on D-Day June 6, 1944. In the Pacific, all during 1944 the U.S. had regained many Pacific Islands from the Japanese in fierce sea and land battles. President Franklin D. Roosevelt had died in office on April 12, 1945 during his 3rd term, and Harry S. Truman was now the President. After successful campaigns by the Allies all over Europe, Germany surrendered on May 7, 1945 on what was designated as V-E Day. Then, following the dropping of the atomic bomb on Hiroshima, Japan also surrendered on V-J Day, August 15, 1945.

The U.S.troops that had survived the war all came home to grand victory parades and tried to pick up their normal lives again. A good thing that a grateful country did for the returning war veterans was to enact a benefits law known as the G.I. Bill of Rights. Among other benefits, this Bill provided for a free college education for any returning war veteran regardless of military rank. My brother Ray benefited from this. He was an Air Force Sargeant who flew on more than 40 missions over Europe in a B-26 bomber as a gunner. He was released from the service in 1947 and went to college at U.C. Berkeley under the G.I. Bill. The original Selective Service Law (the Draft) expired in 1947; so I had in effect escaped being in the service.

JOB HUNTING - 1946

During my last semester of college in the Spring of 1946, I had applied to numerous companies and gone on several interviews in an effort to line up a good job as an engineer upon my graduation from Texas A&M. Most of the possibilities were in the central large cities of Texas. However, in spite of the demand for engineers and my graduation from a top University, nothing concrete materialized. I didn't land a job. Discrimination against Mexican-Americans in Texas was still evident.

At the time, I was not worried about this because I had a promise for a job from El Paso Electric Company. This had come about because I had worked for them during the Summer of 1943 as a Substation laborer. The Superintendent, Jack Stewart, had befriended me and he kept in contact with me by mail while I was away at school. He encouraged me to finish my engineering education, and it was because of his intercession that the Company had agreed to hire me as an engineer after I graduated. So upon my return to El Paso, Mr. Stewart arranged an interview for me with the Company Chief Engineer. However, things did not turn out well. The job that was offered me was a technician's job, testing meters. I turned it down because this was not the engineer's job that had been promised me. Mr. Stewart agreed with me, and he was furious at the Company for their apparent bias toward me. I, of course was disappointed and hurt at this rejection; it also meant that I did not have any immediate prospects for a job. What was I to do now? I did what I've done all my life; I prayed and asked the Lord for His help.

SAN FRANCISCO

That Summer of 1946, Antonia, my sister (by now we called her Toni), who worked at Hotel Dieu Hospital in El Paso, was offered a better paying job at Mary's Help Hospital in San Francisco, California. Both hospitals were run by the Sisters of Mercy. Since I was without a job and because I wanted to get away from the prejudice and discrimination of the Southwest, I decided to go to San Francisco with Toni.

We arrived in San Francisco by bus on August 1, 1946. A family named Gonzalez, whom we had known from our Westwood days, allowed us to stay with them for a short while. One of the Gonzalez' was a boy about my age named Rudy; we became immediate friends. The Gonzalez family of five adults lived in a three bedroom flat on Oak Street near Fillmore. Needless to say, with the addition of two more people, these quarters were crowded.

However, Toni soon started her new job and, shortly thereafter, she and I moved to 554 Waller Street. We rented a room there from a lady from San Salvador, who owned the two flat building.

I got my first job through an employment agency. It was with Pacific Electric Manufacturing Company (PEM) which was located on Third Street in the Bayview district. I started there on about September 1, 1946 in the Engineering department for $200 a month. This Company designed and manufactured high voltage electrical switchgear for electric utility companies throughout the country. I was on the drafting board and although this was not what I wanted to do for long, at least I had a job and was gaining some experience. Nevertheless, I continued to look around and check with other prospective employers. As a result, in the Spring of 1947, the Bureau of Reclamation in Denver, Colorado offered me a position as a design engineer in their North Platte River area where they were constructing a large hydro project.

This Bureau job offer was for more pay than what I was receiving at PEM; additionally, the position seemed to offer better advancement possibilities. After a lot of thought, I accepted. My plan was to quit my job at PEM and report to Denver one month hence. However in the ensuing days, this decision caused me a lot of turmoil because in the preceding months I had met a young girl who was my girlfriend - sort of. The following clarifies this.

COURTSHIP DAYS

In the Fall of 1946, Rudy Gonzalez and I used to go to public dances at various dance halls in San Francisco and

Oakland. Rudy had a steady girlfriend and since I didn't have any other friends, I tagged along with them to parties and dances. On a memorable Sunday night in late August, 1946, I was at Sweet's Ballroom in Oakland just listening to the music, talking with Rudy, and watching others dance. Unexpectedly, something happened that changed my entire life!

A slender, young, and beautiful girl, dressed stylishly, came up to me and asked in a soft voice:

"Excuse me, but are you from El Paso ?"

You could have knocked me over with a feather! I had never seen this girl before, but when she mentioned El Paso, I immediately looked upon her as a long lost friend. It was as if someone had thrown me a life preserver in the sea of loneliness. I certainly wanted to find out more about this "brazen" young woman who had approached me, a perfect stranger.

Our subsequent introductions indicated that her name was **Alicia Evangeline Ramirez.** She was from Tucumcari, New Mexico, but after graduating from high school there, she had lived in El Paso for several years. She had seen me playing there with the Swing Kings Orchestra at the Cortez Hotel. So when she saw me in Oakland that night, somehow she felt compelled to talk to me, even though we had never met. Well, I was happy to see someone from back home, so of course I asked her to dance. She was a good dancer and we danced together all night, even though she claimed she had a date with another fellow there that night. I didn't take her home that evening, since her escort for the night was her uncle Polo, but she did agree to a date with me for the following evening. She had made such a powerful impression on me that I could hardly wait for the next day to come.

Alicia lived in San Francisco with her parents at 974 Minnesota Street in the Potrero District. The following evening I was late for our date, because I was new in the city and didn't know how to get around on the Muni bus lines. I wound up in Hunters Point, but I backtracked and finally got to her house. Her parent's house was a three story building with three flats; the Ramirez family lived in the middle flat. When I got there I was met at the door by a small girl in pigtails (Alicia's younger sister, Rita) who gave me a critical look and then asked: "Are you Catholic?" I was taken aback by this query, but I guess I passed the initial inspection because Rita let me in the door.

After meeting Alicia's family, which consisted of her father Selso Ramirez, her mother Maria Gavina, her sister Rita Lydia, and her grandmother Francisca Rivera Roybal, we set out to go on our first date. I, of course wanted to make a good impression, but I goofed. We went to a bar on Kearny Street where I ordered a beer and Alicia ordered a soft drink. But I could tell she wasn't comfortable there, so we left immediately and went to the movies at a theatre on Market Street. Now she was happier because she loved the movies. When I took her home that night, I asked, "when can I see you again?" She was very noncommittal but finally agreed to another date the following weekend.

The Fall and Winter of 1946 was a period when Alicia and I were together more and more. I thoroughly enjoyed her company and I could see right off that this girl was different from any that I had previously known. She was full of fun, had a strong character, and had a demeanor that commanded a lot of respect. I was determined to know her better. The frequency of our dates and meetings went from bi-weekly, to weekly, and then to twice-a-week. I perceived that she enjoyed going out with me, but in those early weeks she never told me that she liked me. I could never elicit any positive feelings from her about our relationship. This was difficult for me, and my patience was tested, but nevertheless, we continued to see each other, and had fun in the process.

During those times I didn't have a car of course, so on our dates we travelled everywhere in the city by bus. A favorite place was Playland-At-The-Beach where we spent hours in the "fun house", and going on the various rides, such as the giant roller coaster, loop-the-loop, ferris wheel, and bumper cars. On many occasions, we were accompanied by Sam and Francis Garcia, a newly married couple whom we enjoyed being with. Francis was Alicia's sister (she was adopted by Alicia's grandmother) and they were very close friends.

On one occasion we borrowed a car from Jake Garcia, Sam's brother. Now I didn't know how to drive, but I wasn't going to admit it. So I drove to the Edgewater Ballroom at Ocean Beach to a dance where a big name orchestra was playing. When we got to the western part of the city the fog was so dense that you couldn't see fifty feet ahead of you. Fortunately we didn't have an accident, but after that, Alicia didn't encourage me to borrow Jake's car any more.

Another favorite place was Golden Gate Park. We spent a lot of time there at attractions where even today, people from all over the world come to see. We visited the aquarium, Japanese Tea Garden, De Young Museum, and

Ocean Beach. Additionally we played tennis in the park, had picnics in the meadows, and strolled along the various pathways and enjoyed the scenery and the flowers.

In general this was a time of my life when I was no longer lonely because I had found someone whose company I thoroughly enjoyed. Life had taken on a new meaning for me, and it seemed that this girl from Tucumcari was constantly in my thoughts, night and day. By Spring of 1947, without realizing it, I had fallen in love with Alicia!

She was unique, and superior in all respects to any other girl I had ever known. I was attracted strongly to her because of her various physical attributes and her reserved sensuality, but her real beauty was in her inner person. She had a calmness and serenity about her that is impossible for me to describe. Also, one could tell that her upbringing, character, and moral standards were exemplary. Now the only problem was, that I wasn't sure how she felt about me. She surely wasn't the demonstrative type, and up to now she hadn't professed any deep affection for me; even though as I have stated, we saw quite a bit of each other, and I could tell that she enjoyed our dates and being with me.

Now you see my dilemma. I had accepted the position with the Bureau of Reclamation in Denver and was due to report April 1, 1947. This job was certain to be better for my career than the one I had in San Francisco, but this would mean not seeing Alicia anymore. If I went to Denver, it most certainly would not help in my quest to win her over to me. I discussed the situation with her, but she was of no help. The decision of course was up to me. So after agonizing about the future, I decided not to report to Denver. Alicia was happy about this, I found out later.

Another action I took that Spring, was a trip to El Paso. Alicia did not want me to go; she suspected something, but I went. My motives were to see if anyone in El Paso still had any attraction for me. I looked up old girlfriends and in my mind compared them to Alicia. There was no comparison. So I returned to San Francisco to my job at PEM, and made up my mind to win over this gal from Tucumcari!

OUR ENGAGEMENT

The natural sequence of events, as determined by the Lord, happened next. On a bright Sunday in early June, 1947, Alicia and I were at the Golden Gate Park main concourse sitting on the grass talking, and listening to the band play. After a lot of "beating around the bush", I finally got up enough courage to ask her to marry me! Much to my joy and ecstacy, Alicia immediately said "yes". Right there, we sealed our pact with a lingering kiss; as young lovers have done through the centuries. I was so happy because up until that moment, I had never been certain that Alicia loved me; now I was sure that our love for each other was mutual.

We were now engaged, and the first order of business Alicia insisted on was that I ask for her "hand" in marriage with her parents. She wanted this "as the proper thing to do", out of respect for them. I was not looking forward to this, because even though my relationship with her folks was good, I didn't know them that well. Nevertheless, on the following evening I was ushered into the Ramirez' living room. I can still remember the scene; I was sitting on one side of the room, and Alicia, her mother, and her father were sitting on the opposite side on a couch, waiting expectantly for me to say something. Her sister, Rita was in the hallway furtively peeking into the room through the doorway. The silence was deafening. Finally I did the best I could and gave a little speech that I had prepared in my head. It was well received by Alicia's parents and they both offered their congratulations amid "abrazos"; the tension was broken and we had her parents' blessing.

Our engagement lasted for about one year. During the ensuing year we had several goals in mind. Besides getting to know each other better, another goal was to save a little money so that we could get married. We both had a job of course, but I didn't have any savings nor wordly possessions. Alicia worked at the American Can Company on Third Street. She was slightly better off than I financially, but not by much, as she helped her mother with the family living expenses. I bought an engagement ring on the installment plan at Gensler & Lee Jewelry store at 22nd & Mission Street for $250. I spent the last penny I had for the down payment, got the ring, and then paid $10 every two weeks for about eight months. I was happy though, because Alicia looked good with the diamond ring on her finger. As the months went by, we both looked forward to our wedding with much anticipation.

By Spring of 1948, Toni and I lived in an apartment at 49 Noe Street in San Francisco. Also brother Raymond was living nearby and going to college at U.C. Berkeley. At the same time he was carrying on a long distance romance with a former classmate of his who lived in Los Angeles. Her name was Consuelo Caballero. Janie was married to a man named Juan Alonzo and they resided in El Paso. Isobel, my sister, was finishing high school and lived with Janie. Amalia, my half sister was also in El Paso and still living with my grandmother, who by then was quite elderly.

(My grandmother, Francisca Ramirez, later died in El Paso on August 2, 1955 at age 89).

OUR WEDDING

As an engaged couple, Alicia and I now spent a lot of time together. We tried to be practical and do things that didn't cost a lot of money ; however, we still managed to enjoy our dates and time together. San Francisco in the late 1940's was a fun place to live. Riding the ferries, seeing the boats and yachts at the Marina, watching the sun set below the Golden Gate Bridge, eating crab salad at Fisherman's Wharf, freezing at Ocean Beach outings, and going to the movies at the elegant Fox and Warfield Theatres on Market street, all have special remembrances for me. On special occasions we would go dancing at the Fairmont Hotel or listen to the Earl Fatha Hines All Stars jazz band at the Club Hangover on Bush Street. Also, occasionally we would go with friends on outings to the Russian River or to Santa Cruz. This was a great time in my life.

We also spent a lot of time at Alicia's home just talking and planning for the future; I have always been a good planner. I especially liked to visit Alicia on Sunday afternoons. Her mother, Gavina, would invite me to stay for the family dinner, and I just loved those home cooked meals. The food smells that came out of that kitchen was a treat in itself, and the tortillas were out of this world.

A facet of our relationship between Alicia and I, and one which I must mention, was the mutual respect that we had developed for one another. It seemed that from the very beginning we were considerate of each other's feelings. At no time did I ever take advantage of our relationship in any physical disrespectful way. We just seemed to have a common (unspoken) understanding about being courteous, and how to conduct ourselves with each other. I guess in this regard we were just lucky to seemingly be so compatible, but at the same time our Christian upbringing, and trust in God, I'm sure helped us during those courtship times.

Alicia and I were married on a Saturday morning, June 12, 1948 in a nuptial mass at St. Teresa's Catholic Church, which is at 390 Missouri Street, in the Potrero District of San Francisco. At the time, I was about 24 years - 5 months of age, and Alicia was about 23 years - 11 months old. By many standards the wedding ceremony was a small one, but it was well attended by family members, other relatives, and many friends, including co-workers from PEM Co. and American Can Co. Ray, my brother, was the best man, and Gloria Burns, who was Alicia's close friend, was the maid of honor. Rita Ramirez, Alicia's sister, and Prospera Gerbo, a friend, were the flower girls.

Alicia was a beautiful looking bride for sure. She looked positively radiant in her long white wedding gown with a train. The gown was made of all lace and had a flared skirt. The dress had a sweetheart neckline and was form fitted around her slender waist and upper body. She carried a bouquet of white stephanotis and orchids. I stood at the altar attired in my new dark blue suit and watched as Alicia walked up the church aisle on the arm of her father. I was a bit nervous, but I knew in my heart that this girl from Tucumcari was the one for me. I offered up a silent, short prayer for my good luck.

After the wedding, a festive but modest reception was held at Alicia's parent's home. There, lots of tasty home prepared food and drinks abounded, amid the well wishes of everyone present. We also received many nice and thoughtful gifts from our friends. Additionally, we had our wedding pictures taken at a photographer's shop near Union Square. We left the reception in the late afternoon and went to the Crest Hotel on Mason Street where we had reserved a very nice room. After dinner at a favorite restaurant of ours, we returned to the hotel where we spent our wedding night. (This hotel was knocked down many years later to make way for the present Hilton Hotel).

HONEYMOON

The next morning, after Sunday Mass at Old St. Mary's Church in Chinatown, we boarded a Southern Pacific train and set out for Los Angeles, where we spent the next two weeks on our blissful honeymoon. We had made reservations at a centrally located hotel in downtown L.A. and it was perfect for us because of the transportation convenience. Neither of us had been to Los Angeles, other than just passing through, so we did a lot of sightseeing. The Pacific Electric rail lines took us to distant places like Santa Monica and Long Beach and Hollywood; each of these treks took up the whole day, but we didn't mind. We also spent many hours at Griffith Park taking in all the attractions there, such as the zoo, the many museums, and flower gardens. We went to Olvera Street to eat good Mexican food and to hear the Mariachis. We visited the RKO radio studios and were selected as participants in a popular daytime quiz show. (All we won was a toaster identical to one we had received as a wedding gift).

One of the highlights of our stay in L.A. was going to the Palladium to hear the Les Brown Orchestra in person. The Palladium was a very famous ballroom and restaurant where the Big Bands of the day played for dances; Les Brown was one of the most popular swing bands in the 1940's. Alicia and I both enjoyed dancing, we were pretty good at "jitterbugging", but on our honeymoon we enjoyed the slow, romantic ballads the best.

It seemed that we went to so many places, that by the end of every day, we returned to our hotel exhausted. Nevertheless, we had a wonderful honeymoon and enjoyed the many shared intimate moments together. It was an awesome feeling for me to be among millions of people, and yet to be conscious of only Alicia at my side.

I should mention that while we were in Los Angeles, we also attended the wedding of my brother Ray, and his fiancee, Consuelo; they were married on the weekend following our wedding.

Well, as the saying goes, all good things must end, so after two blissful honeymoon weeks in Los Angeles, Alicia and I returned to San Francisco to continue our married life. Alicia had gained six pounds on our honeymoon; I guess married life was already agreeing with her. However, since Alicia was tall and had a slender body, the extra pounds just made her look all the more attractive.

Our first home was the front apartment at 972 Minnesota Street which was one of the flats of the building owned by Alicia's parents. Despite my objections, we payed no rent; her mother wanted us to save money so that we could eventually buy our own house. This was a very generous deal and a big help financially. I was only making about $250/month at work, and we had decided that Alicia was not going to work anymore, as we wanted to start a family soon. In fact, she predicted that we were going to have six children! I humored her about this, but didn't give her comment any further thought.

I was now a married man with a wife. Once again I was at another major plateau in my young life, except that now I had a partner. **Getting married was the single most important event in my entire life.** It changed my whole future. At the time I thanked the Lord for Alicia. I could now see His hand in the torturous road I had travelled for over 22 years before He put me at Sweet's Ballroom in Oakland, where Alicia and I met on that fateful day in August, 1946. And so I looked to the future filled with hope and faith in the Lord.

7
Family and Career

MARRIED LIFE

Alicia and I settled in and adapted to our domestic married life quite easily. However, materially we did not have much; we had few wordly possessions. Alicia had bought a bedroom set prior to our marriage with her own money, so at least we had that. Also, we had received many useful wedding gifts such as pots and pans, utensils, and bed coverings. All I brought to our apartment was my own clothes. We had no bank account. We did not own a T.V. set because they were very expensive. In 1948, television broadcasting was in its infancy. We used to occasionally visit a friend of ours who did have a T.V. set. It must have cost a fortune. The set had a tiny nine inch picture tube and was housed in a huge entertainment center. A plastic magnifying glass for better viewing was mounted in front of the picture tube, but external to the set. You can imagine the distortion that this caused in the picture.

Nevertheless, the months following our wedding were very happy ones for me as a lot of my efforts were directed towards loving and cherishing my new bride. As I suspected, Alicia was an excellent homemaker and cook. When I got home from work she always had dinner ready. I can still picture her in that tiny aroma filled kitchen standing in front of the gas stove with her apron on. At first I was apprehensive about living so close to Alicia's parents and family, but this did not prove to be any problem for us. Her family was very supportive of us, but at the same time they did not interfere in our married life in any way. Alicia and I continued to do the things that we both enjoyed, like going to the movies, attending dances at the El Patio Ballroom at Market and Van Ness, listening to jazz at the Club Hangover on Bush Street, and going on picnics and outings with our friends.

From the very beginning Alicia and I resolved to continue practicing our Catholic faith. Our total commitment was to each other but always under the acknowledgment of the presence of the Lord. What helped to point us in this direction, besides our upbringing, was a pre-marital series of lectures that we had attended at Old St. Mary's Church in Chinatown. These practical lectures were given by the Paulist Fathers and made quite an impression on us. They covered many aspects of spiritual and sexual teachings of the Catholic faith.

WE START A FAMILY

Very soon after we were married Alicia became pregnant. Subsequently, on Friday, April 8, 1949 at 4:56 pm at Mary's Help Hospital on Guerrero Street in San Francisco, our first born came into this world. It was a boy. He weighed seven pounds, one and a half ounces, and was nineteen and a half inches long. We named our son Jess Alvino Herrera, after his father and grandfather. The attending physician was Dr. H.F. Schwarz. Becoming a father for the first time was an awesome feeling hard to describe. Needless to say I was elated and very happy at this blessed event and I passed out cigars and candy to friends and acquaintances at work. I might add that our total cost was $125 for a private doctor, which covered pre-natal care and a normal delivery, plus $117 for the six day stay at the hospital for Alicia and the baby. Soon thereafter on June 19th, Jess was baptized at St Teresa's Catholic Church. Toni Herrera, my sister, and Rudy Gonzalez, a friend, were the Godparents.

As any parent can relate to, our son's arrival into this world changed our lives dramatically. Now instead of two adults catering to each other to make a marriage work, the focus of attention shifted to a small baby. We went about our new job of parenting, learning as we went along. I saw Alicia in a completely new light. She was amazing. She seemed to know instinctively how to take care of baby Jess. It took me a long time to get over the wonder and awe of having a son and starting a family, but I resolved to do my best as now I had an additional and major responsibility. In June, 1949 we celebrated our first wedding anniversary. I felt blessed that that the first year of my new life had gone so good.

On October 31, 1950 I became a proud father for the second time. Albert Anthony Herrera, a son weighing seven pounds - eight ounces, was born at Mary's Help Hospital in San Francisco on Halloween night. When I saw

Alicia following the delivery she said: "We have a cute little spook." The baby's name was chosen because we liked the name "Albert"; it had a regal sound to it. Anthony was chosen as the middle name to honor St. Anthony who was Alicia's favorite saint to pray to when she needed special favors. Additionally, it was a family name because of Antonia, my sister. Dr. Schwarz, our family obstretician, was the attending physician. Baby Albert was baptized on December 10, 1950 at St. Teresa's Catholic Church; his grandmother, Gavina Ramirez, was the sole Godparent.

Our family was growing. Now we had two sons fairly close together in age. I was happy about this because I figured that as they grew up they would be good company for each other. Also, I felt a family pride in that it assured that the Herrera name would be perpetuated; at least for another generation. Having two babies in the house made our lives a little more complex. But having Alicia at home at all times was a Godsend. I tried to help Alicia with the early care for the babies as much as I could, although I was always fearful of sticking them with the safety pins when changing their diapers (we didn't have disposable diapers in those days). However, I really enjoyed playing with the babies and seeing them develop. One thing I never did get used to though, was the short hours of nightly sleep that I got. I'm a person that needs lots of sleep. So the nightly feedings and times when the babies were sick took it's toll on me. I am sure that all parents can relate to what I'm talking about.

Another change that took place about this time was that I bought our first car. We needed it to get around with our growing family, especially for checkup visits for our sons with Dr. McPhee, the pediatrician. The car was an eight year old 1942 Chevrolet, light green in color, four door, with a floor mounted stick shift. This car served us well and we kept it about four years before it gave out and we had to replace it. It was during this period that I got my driver's license, and out of necessity, learned how to maintain and repair a car. In this regard I learned quite a bit from Sam Garcia, as he was always ready to help me tune up the car, change the engine oil, or replace the spark plugs.

JOB CHANGE

In the meantime my career at Pacific Electric Manufacturing Company (PEM) was progressing but at a pretty slow pace. I received some periodic salary increases but since this was a relatively small Company, the promotional opportunities did not exist. Many of the engineers at PEM were top experts in their field and well known in the electrical power industry. These key people were pretty well set in their positions and movement from below was practically impossible. Another major misgiving that I had about my job was that most of the basic engineering being done here was mechanical in nature rather than electrical, which was my specialty.

Nevertheless, in spite of these drawbacks, I learned a lot about the engineering and manufacturing business in general and specifically about electrical power switchgear equipment while at PEM. Also, an advantage of being with a small Company was that the job assignments were quite varied. These experiences all came in handy later on in my career. I actually enjoyed my associations with PEM people; they were friendly and professional. To this day I occasionally still run across a few remaining friends from the old PEM days.

After being at PEM for about five years, I realized that with a growing family I needed to go in a new direction with my career as an engineer. So I decided to look for another job. This was during late Summer 1951.

EARLY CAREER AT PACIFIC GAS & ELECTRIC COMPANY (P.G.& E.)

The best fit for my interests was with Pacific Gas and Electric Company (P.G.& E.), whose headquarters were in San Francisco. So I applied there, and after several very exhaustive interviews, was subsequently offered two jobs. One of the jobs offered was as a Construction Field Engineer. But this job required long stays in the field throughout Northern and Central California. In fact my first assignment was to be at Humboldt Bay Power plant in Eureka, California. I could not accept this job because of my young family. So I accepted the second job offered even though it required that I be on the drafting board once again. I started at P.G.& E. on September 3, 1951. My first position was as a Draftsman "A" in the Design-Drafting Department, General Office, at 245 Market Street in San Francisco.

P.G.& E. is the largest investor owned gas and electric utility in the U.S. Its 94,000 square mile service territory covers most of Northern and Central California - an area that includes 48 of the state's 58 counties with a population of almost 12 million people. As of this writing the Company has over 26,000 employees.

In 1951, the Company was embarking on a massive electric and natural gas facility expansion program. These additional facilities were needed to accommodate the post World War 2 economic expansion that was going on in

California. Thousands of people from other states were settling in California every day. Business was booming and the people at P.G.& E. were busy planning, designing, and constructing gas facilities, electrical substations, and fossil and hydro-electric power plants. So I looked forward to working in this environment with eager anticipation as I wanted to not only advance my professional career, but also to provide a stable employment base for the good and future of my family.

I was assigned to an electrical design squad whose product was drawings suitable for construction of various Company facilities and structures. At that time in the General Office, all graduate engineers started with the Company in the Drafting Department before being considered for a higher position in the more prestigious "Engineering Department." So I didn't mind being on the drafting board at first since all around me were graduate engineers from universities like Stanford and U.C. Berkeley.

My first job was to design and specify the high voltage equipment for Transformer Bank No. 3 at Moraga Substation in the East Bay area of San Francisco. My supervisors found out that I knew about wiring diagrams, control systems, and protective relaying schemes so I was soon the squad "expert" in those areas. I particularly liked the engineering application and theory of electrical power equipment. However, my job description also required that I make drawings from which something could be built. My mechanical drawing and lettering skills were passable but this was not my forte; nevertheless the drawings were accurate and understandable. Soon thereafter I was promoted to the grade of Designer B, then later to Designer A.

As an electrical Designer "A" I worked very closely, on many projects, with the Project Electrical Engineers from the Engineering Department. These engineers were an elite group of individuals that because of their seniority or expertise, had the responsibility for the proper engineering and design of the construction drawings, as well as specifying all the major equipment. Actually there were two formal Electrical Engineering Departments in the Company; Distribution and Transmission. Each group was headed up by a Chief Engineer and each had under him about a dozen engineers who did the electrical system planning and ran the projects.

Murphys Powerhouse was one of the most interesting projects that I worked on in those early days. This project was a new hydro facility in the Sierra foothills. I worked with a senior engineer named Frank Lawson on this job and he gave me a lot of freedom regarding the design of the project. The powerhouse was an unattended, completely automatic plant with a single generating unit. After its construction, I was also involved in the field testing of the unit to make sure that it ran according to the specifications. I must say that it was a big thrill for me to stand there on the generator floor and watch the unit start from a standstill and run for the first time, and then generate electricity, all without local intervention; i.e. the control was all done remotely via signals from an operating center about 25 miles away. Since I had devised all the automatic control circuits for this project, the successful outcome was very satisfying.

Another major achievement for me was in 1954 when I acquired my California Professional Engineers Registration License. My License No. is Electrical E-5276. It took me many hours of self-study at home and a lot of determination to pass the tough day-long written examination. The reason I became registered was because I aspired to be promoted to the Engineering Department and professional registration was a prerequisite.

My job at P.G.& E. progressed nicely during 1952 thru 1954 and I made many close friends from among my fellow workers. However, as time went on I was getting impatient that I was not being promoted to the Engineering Department, even though I was doing good work and openings were available. Several of the Supervising Engineers in the Transmission Engineering Department had recommended that I be promoted, but for some reason it wasn't happening. I couldn't even get an appointment with W.R.Johnson, the Chief Engineer, to plead my own case. I was beginning to wonder whether some form of prejudice was again rearing it's ugly head. I felt that I had now reached another plateau in my career and was ready for another move.

Finally by a stroke of good fortune, Clive Baugh, the Chief Engineer of the Distribution Engineering Department, offered me a job as an Electrical Engineer in the Substation Group. Thus in May, 1956, I was out of the Drafting Room after almost five years with P.G.& E.

Substation Engineering was fairly easy work for me compared to Generation or Transmission engineering, which is what I had been doing. Mentally the work wasn't very stimulating but it did give me some additional experience in another facet of utility engineering. Equally as important was the fact that my salary had been increased to about $550 a month. Additionally, being in the Engineering Department resulted in many subtle attitude changes towards me from others within and outside the Company.

It was surprising in those days, how status conscious people were. The engineers within the Company were held in high esteem and engineering was a good career path at P.G.& E. I suppose this was because the successful completion of the capital intensive construction program depended heavily upon engineers.

FAMILY LIFE IN THE EARLY 1950'S

By January, 1952, Alicia and I had saved enough money to make the down payment on our first house. The house we bought was at 178 Farallones Street in the Ocean View District of San Francisco. The house was a fairly new one with three bedrooms and a full basement including a garage. The house cost $13,200 and the down payment was $4,200. We managed to save this large amount from my salary by putting aside almost $100 every month ever since we were married. Our monthly mortgage payment were $70 per month and the loan was at five percent interest rate. We were still on a very tight budget because we also had to buy additional furniture; but somehow we got by. However, to help meet our monthly house, tax and insurance payments, and other expenses, I took on a second job by teaching night classes at Healds College on Van Ness Avenue twice a week for about three years. At various times I taught AC and DC basic electricity subjects, drafting, and different levels of math subjects such as algebra, trigonometry and calculus.

On January 31, 1955 at about 4:00 a.m. we were blessed with the birth of of our first daughter. Gloria Alicia Herrera was born at Mary's Help Hospital. She weighed 8 pounds - 3 ounces and had a lot of very black hair. Once again Doctor H. Schwarz was the attending physician. I was thrilled to have a baby girl in our family. I now had two sons and a daughter, which I thought was a good combination for a family. I was 31 years of age. We chose the name Gloria to glorify God and we also wanted a name that was spelled the same in English and Spanish. The middle name was chosen to perpetuate Alicia's name in our first born daughter. Later, on March 13, 1955, Gloria was baptized at St. Michaels Catholic Church on Broad Street. Sam and Francis Garcia were the Godparents.

An episode that comes to mind when I recall Gloria's birth is the following: About a week before the baby was due I made sure that Alicia and I were fully prepared to go to the hospital. Alicia had her bag packed and I had the car full of gas and ready, just waiting for the right moment. Along about 11:00 pm on January 30th, I got the word from Alicia that her time had come. So we ran down to the garage, got into the car, and started to go. It was then that I realized that the strange hissing sound I was hearing was a flat tire. I stopped at a nearby Union 76 service station at Alemany and Broad Street. The station had just closed but I cajoled the attendant to open up. I promised him a big tip if he would fix the tire in a hurry. He fixed it in record time, mainly I believe, because he didn't want a baby born right there by his gas pumps. He kept glancing at Alicia all during the tire fixing. I was a mental wreck by the time we got to the hospital; but of course Alicia was her usual calm self all during this time. Also Gloria didn't come into this world until hours later. This "famous" gas station was torn down many years later, but to this day whenever I pass that intersection I think of that event which happened many years ago.

FAMILY KEEPS GROWING

By late Summer, 1956, Alicia informed me that she was expecting again. By now I was used to this and didn't mind at all because I felt that this is what the Lord had destined for me. Besides I reasoned that if the new baby was a girl then we would have a nicely balanced family of two boys and two girls. But of course it didn't turn out this way.

On March 11, 1957, Alicia gave birth to twin boys at Kaiser Hospital on Geary Street in San Francisco. When the nurse came out of the delivery room and told me that I had a son I was very happy of course. But when she came out again a minute later and told me about the second newborn baby I was flabbergasted, as twins were totally unexpected. In those days prior knowledge about the nature of the fetus before birth was meager, unlike today's full knowledge with modern medical scanning techniques.

The first born twin was Robert and the second was Michael. They each weighed about five pounds - three ounces. However tragedy struck. It turned out that Robert was born with a kidney malfunction and he died in the hospital two days later. Alicia and I were devastated at this turn of events, but eventually accepted Robert's death as God's will. He was baptized in the hospital by a priest before he expired and so we know that we have an angel in heaven interceding for us Herreras who still remain on this earth. During those trying days we were also consoled by the fact that Michael was quite healthy and thriving in this world outside Alicia's womb. I immediately arranged for Robert's burial at Holy Cross Catholic Cemetery in Colma; he was buried in the same grave with Alicia's father, Selso, who had died in 1956. Just a few immediate family members were present at the gravesite; Alicia, still in the hospital and grief stricken, could not attend. I shall forever remember Robert. We gave him his name from my middle name.

Michael Selso Herrera was baptized on April 8, 1957 at St. Michaels Catholic Church. Rita (Alicia's sister) and Henry Arias (Rita's husband) were the Godparents. It was appropriate that my son be baptized in this church because we named him after St. Michael the Archangel. His middle name, Selso, is for his maternal grandfather. Now two of our sons, Michael and Jess, have their grandfather's names in their names. When I think about how Michael survived and his twin brother didn't, I know that God gave Michael life to bring joy, happiness, and protection to those family members around him.

We lived on Farallones Street until May, 1957. By that time Jess and Albert were in grade school at Sheridan public school. We made a decision to sell our house after living there for about five years because we felt that the neighborhood was not a good and stable place in the long term, to raise our young family. We sold the house at a small profit but had to carry a second mortgage in order to sell it. Once again my mother-in-law, Gavina Ramirez, helped us out. She was living on Connecticut Street in the Potrero Hill area of San Francisco, and she allowed us to live in a basement apartment there until we could find another home. The apartment was tiny and the six of us barely fit into it.

Also, it turned that by this time Alicia was pregnant once again. I had not planned to have another baby so soon because I was concerned about Alicia's health. After all she was already raising four young children and it had been less than a year since Michael was born. Fortunately, her health held up and her enthusiasm was great, so I eagerly looked forward to another addition to our family.

My fourth son, Richard Ray Herrera, was born on February 2, 1958, at Kaiser Hospital in San Francisco. We chose his name because we liked the sound of it; the middle name was that of my brother Raymond. I was very happy at the birth of another boy in the family. I reasoned that perhaps he and his brother Michael, being nearly the same age, would be close friends during the various stages of their lives. When we brought baby Richard home from the hospital, there was no room in that tiny apartment to put his crib. We finally found a niche for him in the kitchen corner; that was his first home, but he was a good baby and did not complain. But it was obvious now that with my large family, we soon had to find a bigger place to live in.

My sister, Isobel, had recently married Vidal Estrada in San Francisco in June, 1956. So we asked them to be Richard's Godparents and they agreed. Richard was baptized on February 23, 1958, at St. Teresa's Catholic Church in San Francisco and he was now a member of the Faith Community of Jesus Christ.

We moved into our present home at 420, 38th Avenue in the Richmond District of San Francisco in March, 1958. Alicia was the one that selected this house from many that she looked at. When I first visited the house I was impressed with the character and solid construction of the house; also, it was the biggest house I had ever been in. It had three floors, with a garage as part of the basement floor. There were also two almost finished rooms in the basement level. I could see that this house would serve our growing family quite well. It was to be our family home.

We bought the house and made a $5,500 down payment. The outstanding loan was to be repaid at six percent interest rate. Our monthly payments, including taxes, insurance, and 1st and 2nd mortgages was about $135 per month. Soon after we moved in we had some termite work done, as well as a few other repairs. These additional items brought our initial cost up to a lot more than we had figured on. But in spite of the heavy debt burden, we managed to meet all our house payments on time. During subsequent years, we continued to make many other major improvements and repairs to the house because it was built in about 1915 and thus required a lot of maintenance. Nevertheless, it has served our family well throughout the years.

One thing I must not forget to do is to mention the role of Alicia's mother, Gavina Ramirez, in our family life. This woman has been a constant help to our family. During each of the children's births she was the one that helped out during the time Alicia was in the hospital and also afterwards while Alicia regained her strength. I don't know how I would have managed without her willing support. She has also helped us financially by letting us live rent free in her houses. Gavina has earned the respect and love of all her children, grandchildren and great grandchildren, and she holds the place of high honor and esteem among us all. She is truly a Saint.

> Post note: The family suffered a great loss on November 27, 1991, as Gavina, my mother-in-law, died of a heart attack in Seton Hospital, Daly City, at the age of 86. She is buried in Holy Cross Catholic Cemetery, Colma, Calif.

MY LAST OFFSPRING

Continuing the saga of the birth of my children, lo and behold, by 1961 Alicia was expecting another child again. Now we had talked about this, and we both wanted another baby to round out our family. But at the same time we realized that Alicia was almost 37 years of age and so we were a little apprehensive about how the pregnancy and childbirth would turn out. Fortunately through the grace of God, everything went well. On September 28, 1961, we were blessed with the birth of a healthy baby girl. She was born at Kaiser Hospital on Geary Street in San Francisco.

We named our new daughter Teresa Ann, in honor of two saints that Alicia had a special devotion to; i.e. St. Teresa of Avila, and St. Anne, Mother of the Blessed Virgin. As with our daughter Gloria, we chose the name Teresa so that it would be spelled the same in English and Spanish.

Teresa was baptized at St. Thomas Apostle Catholic Church in San Francisco on November 5, 1961. Raymond Herrera, my brother, and his wife Consuelo, were the Godparents.

Being 37 years of age at the time, I remember that one of my concerns when Teresa was born was whether I was too old and set in my ways to thoroughly enjoy our new born baby. My fears proved groundless of course as Teresa was a great joy to me, Alicia, and the rest of the children during her growing years. As the years went by I appreciated her presence in our family more and more. God was good to me when He gave us Teresa, our youngest. Also, Alicia's prophecy of having six children was fulfilled. I suddenly realized that I should have paid attention to her many years previous, when she had mentioned that we were destined to have six children.

Of course now that I had a large family, a challenge that faced me was to provide support for them. Besides our mortgage and house expenses, we had other major expenses too; such as clothes, car, healthcare, food, and education. I'll talk more about my committment to a quality education for all of my children later. But you see, I had to keep my nose to the grindstone to support my family. Nevertheless, I was determined to do my best so that my family could be raised in a better environment and have better opportunities than I had. I also realized that I was lucky. I had a steady job, and Alicia was a superb wife and mother. So I hoped that with God's help, the high plateaus of life that I was reaching for, were attainable for me and my family.

8
The Middle Years

CAREER NOTES - PROJECT ENGINEERING

After only nine months in the Distribution Engineering Department at Pacific Gas & Electric Company, I was transferred to the Generation and Transmission Engineering Department in February 1957. This was ironic, as this was the same department under W.R. Johnson that had not wanted me only a few months prior. They were now admitting tacitly, that they needed my expertise in the generation area. Nevertheless, I was happy to make this move because the work was certain to be more interesting. I was assigned to work on the engineering for hydro-electric plants. These plants were the most important projects that the Company had underway at the time. Major hydro developments were starting in the Feather River and Kings River areas of California, each involving many plants. Never before in the history of the Company had P.G.& E. undertaken such ambitious and expensive hydro-electric work.

There were only six electrical engineers working on all these projects. Consequently each of us had a large workload and had full responsibility for one or more hydro plants. The work involved specifications for all equipment, facility design, and follow up during construction, and field testing. This was a major challenge for me as it required the application of sound engineering principles, innovative thinking, independent decision making, sound management of resources and schedules, and collaborative working with many other disciplines and people. I was confident in my capabilities and was eager to prove my worth to my bosses.

During the next seven years I was heavily involved in many hydro projects on the Feather River, Kings River, Stanislaus River, and various other locations in Northern and Central California. My experience base was growing and I was given more and more responsibility. I was assigned as Project Electrical and Mechanical Engineer for the new unit additions at Balch Powerhouse, and for the underground powerhouse at Haas Powerhouse. Both of these plants were situated in the Sierra Nevada Mountains east of Fresno, and were large multi-million dollar ventures. I had to solve many difficult engineering and environmental problems to help these plants come "on line". I was extremely happy when these plants were later completed and successfully producing electricity.

Haas Powerhouse is a unique plant in that it is in a huge cavern inside a granite mountain, several hundred feet below the surface of the earth. Many years later I took Michael and Richard on a fishing trip to the Kings River.

We stayed at Company facilities and had a lot of fun "roughing it". On that trip we visited the Haas Powerhouse which was an impressive experience for the boys. They felt it was scary to be underground inside a mountain, with the sounds of whirling machinery and rushing water all around them. I still remember how relieved they were to emerge to the surface.

Another phase of the work during those Hydro plant days was the field testing. I spent many months in the field working with the construction field engineers checking out and testing all the equipment. This meant, of course, that I wasn't at home helping Alicia take care of our family. I didn't particularly like this, but it was part of my job. Nevertheless, Alicia never complained. She deserves a lot of credit for running the family and house while I was away from home. I missed my family a lot during those times, especially during the Christmas seasons. Often I would come home for only a day or for a few hours, just to see everyone; then I would have to go back to the field. The work hours were very long. When testing, it was not unusual to work 16 to 20 hours a day.

By the middle 1960's, most of the major hydro developments were essentially complete. However, a new major transmission line project was now the focus of the Company's attention. This was the 500 kilovolt (kv) transmission line that was to be built from the Pacific Northwest to Southern California. P.G.& E. had a major involvement and financial stake in this project. Besides the new transmission line, several major 500 kv electrical substations were to be built as part of the project.

In 1963 I was transferred to the Planning Section of the department. This Section was the electrical "think tank" of the Company and was heavily involved in the 500 kv project. They were making the analytical and computer studies involving the electrical power system. I was surprised that I was asked to join the group because, even though I had experience with power systems, I did not know very much about computers.

Nevertheless, I was happy about this move because it showed confidence by the Chief Engineer in my ability to take on a new assignment. Little by little I was getting past W.R. Johnson's reticence towards me and other minorities. At that time I was the only Hispanic in the Engineering department. And based on the record to date, it looked impossible for a Mexican American to be in a Corporate position of high responsibility. I didn't ponder much about this, but I continued in my determination to get ahead at P.G.& E., but only if my qualifications warranted it.

CAREER PROMOTIONS

Shortly thereafter, I was promoted to Senior Electrical Engineer. I was very happy about this of course, but at the same time it was my nature to be a little impatient that it had taken me almost eight years of being in the Engineering department to get this recognition. On the other hand I surely needed the increase in salary to support my large family. So I was satisfied for now.

Following two years experience in the Planning Department working on various projects involving computer analysis of power systems, I was moved back once again into design work. I was placed in charge of design work involving all thermal power plants for the department. Additionally during the period between 1965 and 1970 I was the Project Engineer for two 500 kv transmission substations; i.e. Metcalf Substation near San Jose, and Midway Substation near Bakersfield. Also I was responsible for major work on Units 6 & 7 at Moss Landing Power Plant, including the transmission switchyard.

Additionally, I was doing pioneering work on a large nuclear plant facility at Diablo Canyon near San Luis Obispo. This was such an important investment for the Company that little did I know that I would be heavily involved in the engineering and licensing for this plant for the next 25 years.

I am very proud of my contributions on all the projects I have worked on, as providing power and electricity for the good of society, in my view, is a worthwhile and satisfying endeavor. And as I travel around California it gives me a lot of satisfaction to see substations, powerplants, and transmission lines that are there and working because of my God given talents and contributions.

By the late 1960's, I was getting to be an important contributing member of the department. Also, agewise I was in my middle 40's and so I was one of the more senior persons in a department that had grown to about 75 members. In June, 1970 I was promoted once again within the department. I was now a Supervising Electrical Engineer in charge of generation projects and power system applications. I directed the activities of about 12 engineers who were in my group. W.R. Johnson was still the Chief Electrical Engineer. He was a brilliant engineer and was a legend within the Company. However, it was his nature to be reserved and aloof with his employees and I was no exception. But by now I knew that he needed me and recognized that I was a key and vital cog in his department. I think that I had finally won his respect.

BACK TO COLLEGE

Despite my excellent and varied work experience up through the late 1960's, once again I had the feeling that I had reached a career plateau. I had been out of college for many years now and despite my efforts to keep up with technology changes, I felt that I needed new skills to get ahead. My job required that solutions be found to problems by means of computers, advanced mathematics, and power system analysis techniques that I needed to know more about. Technology was passing me by. I didn't know how to cope with this feeling as nobody was complaining about my work; in fact my boss thought I was doing well. Nevertheless I was restless.

So what did I do? I decided that education was to be the answer for me once again. So I enrolled in a Graduate Engineering Program at the University of Santa Clara. However, this time the conditions were vastly different. I was 45 years old and had been out of school for 23 years. Furthermore, I was married, had a wife and six children, and had the responsibilities of a full time job. Also, all classes were held at night. Because of these factors, this task that I undertook was very difficult for me. Fortunately, the Company paid for tuition and book expenses. It took a lot of study time, dedication, perseverance, hard work, and encouragement and understanding from my wife and children, for me to be able to finish this program. However, to this day I still feel pangs of remorse, that the time spent studying was precious time taken away from my family while they were growing up. I sincerely hope they didn't suffer too much because of this.

It took me five years of going to classes at night, taking two classes a quarter, to finish the required program. Finally on June, 1974 I was awarded a Master of Science in Engineering Degree from the University of Santa Clara. I was a very proud person that sunny day at the University graduation ceremonies when I received my diploma. I consider this academic effort one of the major achievements of my life. But it emphasizes the importance I have placed on acquiring a formal education in order to broaden oneself. However, I got my Masters Degree the hard way, and I don't particularly recommend this method to anyone in their late 40's.

ANOTHER CAREER PLATEAU REACHED

Getting a Masters Degree gave my career at P.G.& E. a shot in the arm. In 1976, the electrical engineering function for the Company was reorganized into only one Electrical Engineering Department under W.R.Johnson, but with three separate Sections; Generation, Transmission, and Distribution. I was promoted to head up the Generation Section. In effect each section head was an Assistant Chief Electrical Engineer. Now I had the responsibility for all electrical engineering work involving generation. The main endeavors of the Company at the time were in geo-thermal work at the Geysers area north of San Francisco, a large hydro pumped storage facility named Helms in the central Sierra Nevada mountains, and continuing work on two very large nuclear units at Diablo Canyon near San Luis Obispo on the central coast of California.

W.R. Johnson, retired from the Company in 1979 after holding the Chief Electrical Engineer position for over 30 years. So guess who took his place. You're right. I was promoted to the position of Chief Electrical Engineer for

Pacific Gas & Electric Company on November 1, 1979. This was a department head level position and a very prestigious one within and outside the Company. I had reached a top plateau in my career. Of course it's very ironic that I replaced the man who many years earlier did not even want me in his department. However, I did not hold a grudge against him as I now considered him a friend. Unfortunately, he had a heart attack and passed away about three years after his retirement.

I was promoted to the Chief's position over several key individuals who had seniority over me and who had high hopes of landing the job. Even though I knew I was qualified, I really didn't think I would be picked. However, it was explained to me that senior management thought I was the best qualified person for the job based on my broad experience, past performance, and leadership qualities. As it turned out, my promotion was well received by almost everyone in the department. The good will accorded me by my peers made me very happy. I was now the boss.

I was 55 years old when I reached this career plateau and fully expected to hold my new position until retirement 10 years hence. My family had grown up by now, as Teresa the youngest was 18 years of age. I had come a long way from my humble beginnings as a first generation Mexican - American, and only God knew what lay ahead for me. I prayed that He would help me fulfill the responsibilities of my new and tough position.

FAMILY PHILOSOPHY

Lest anyone think that enhancement of my career was my burning obsession in life, let me assure the reader that it wasn't. To me, my family is the most important and precious gift that I have received. My love for each member of the family is infinite. During the children's growing years, both Alicia and I were committed to providing love, nourishment, good example, and a stable home life for them. We wanted each of them to develop their character, their personality, and their natural talent, all within a rough framework of our own beliefs, traditions and conduct codes. We tried to instill in them traits that we felt were important, such as love for family and God, respect for others, hard work, self-esteem and self-confidence, and responsibility.

I believe that we were successful to a certain degree in accomplishing the above, but this may be only a parent's short term view. All I can say is that we tried our best to show them the way toward the future.

In my case, I continue to reflect on the very positive influence that my parents had on my development and conduct throughout life; even though I was only four years old when my father died and only twelve when my mother died. I hope that all of my children have a similar good feeling towards Alicia and I.

FAMILY EDUCATION

By the time Gloria was born in 1955, Jess was starting kindergarten school. It was during this time that Alicia and I resolved that all of our children were to get the best education possible within our means. This was to be a top priority in our lives. We could see the long term benefits for them in the quality of their lives if we could provide the opportunity and motivation for them to receive a good education. Furthermore, since I was a college graduate, I was determined that every one of my children get the opportunity to go to college and hopefully graduate.

So it turned out that all of our children attended parochial grade school at St. Thomas Apostle school, which was in our neighborhood. We wanted them to get a good foundation in the Catholic faith and this seemed like the best way to do it. We got a break in the tuition charges as all fees were on a per family basis. The kids were given a lot of homework assignments, which they did faithfully most of the time. As a result, their academic grades were pretty good.

Also as I recall, the priests and sisters made sure that everyone was involved in school activities of one form or another; this applied to the parents as well as the kids. As a result I spent a lot of my free time on weekends and nights in support of school activities. As a matter of fact I was president of the St. Thomas Men's Club for a period of time. Thus, I was involved in various things like fund raising, laying out the sports programs, driving kids to baseball and basketball games, and helping with the furniture moving at bazaars and school plays. I was very proud of my children as they graduated, one by one, from the school's eighth grade. High school was next.

Jess, Albert, Michael, and Richard all attended and graduated from St. Ignatius Catholic High School in San Francisco, which was an all boy's school in those days. They each had to pass an entrance examination to get into this college prep school and I remember how relieved and happy we all were when each boy was accepted. Gloria graduated from Star of the Sea Academy, which was an all girl's Catholic high school on Geary Boulevard. Teresa graduated from Mercy High School on 19th Avenue in the city, which also was an all girl's Catholic school.

Finally, I want to record here that all of my children

did attend and graduate from college. Jess graduated from U.C. Berkeley with an MBA degree in marketing. Albert has several degrees including a PhD in biology from U.C. Los Angeles. Gloria holds a BA degree from San Francisco State University in radio and television (magna cum laude). Michael got his BS degree in engineering technology from Cal Poly, San Luis Obispo. Richard graduated from U.C. Berkeley with a BA degree in architecture, and Teresa is a graduate of Cal Poly, San Luis Obispo and U.C. Davis with BS and MS degrees in civil engineering.

The north wall of the dining room in our house is a place of family honor and distinction for education. All the college diplomas in our family are on exhibit there. This includes mine, our children's, and the boys' spouse's diplomas. I call it "THE WALL OF FAME". Alicia and I are very proud of these diplomas since it is the culmination of our dreams and sacrifices for a quality education for our children. Also, each of these diplomas represents a lot of hard work and dedication on the part of my sons and daughters, and others; they should be very proud of their achievements. It's something worthwhile they did and they deserve our accolades.

Sending the children to all these schools was quite expensive for us, but this is where our top priority was for channelling our money. Thank God we made it through. Also, I should mention that each of our sons and daughters contributed some money of their own toward their schooling expenses by working at various odd jobs throughout their growing years. When they were older, a big help money wise was the P.G.& E. summer jobs that they got through my intercession at work. These jobs paid them good wages and gave them some experience working in the offices or doing manual labor in the field.

FAMILY LIFE

As I look back, I realize that a happy and memorable time in my life was during the 1960's. This is because the 1960's was when all my children were at home and we were functioning as a family. We went through the various stages of rearing a family that were typical of the times for those days. Even though I had a large family, somehow we all got along pretty good as the kids were going through the growing phases of their lives. They were active in their school activities, developing friends, and helping around the house. A few typical memories of this period follow:

The kitchen and breakfast room areas of our house were remodeled in 1962. That was a major disruption to our family life. For weeks we used a basement room as a substitute place to cook and eat. Alicia cooked the meals on an electric hot plate and we ate huddled around card tables. No one seemed to complain however, and the younger kids, especially, thought this was all great fun. Upstairs, dust was everywhere. To save money I did a lot of the work like tearing down walls, all the electrical wiring work, and the painting; the contractor did the rest. I can still remember how hard Jess and Albert worked in carrying out the plaster, old lumber, and general debris from the kitchen out to a throwaway box on the street.

It was during dinner time one evening while we were in our basement room that President John F. Kennedy came on T.V. to tell the U.S. people that a serious Soviet Union missile crises was at hand in Cuba. I was quite concerned about this but fortunately the Soviets backed down from a major confrontation with the U.S. and war was averted. However the "cold war" with Communist

Soviet Union was on.

President Kennedy was a very popular president who took office on January 20, 1961. I am a registered Democrat but usually vote the Republican ticket because the Republican Party is more conservative in their taxing and spending policies. However, I voted for Kennedy, even though he was a Democrat, because of his youthful ideas. When he was assassinated in Dallas in November, 1963, I and millions of other Americans were grief stricken and sad. I remember that my first impulse upon hearing of his death was to go to church to pray for him and for our nation; I did this right away.

Another family memory I have about this period of my life was that on nice warm days, usually in late summer, after work I would go directly to Golden Gate Park Lindley Meadows where the whole family was waiting for me. There we would have a baseball game or hit tennis balls with racquets, before mealtime. Then we would have hot dogs, hamburgers, and corn on the cob that Alicia had prepared for us on the outdoor barbeque grills. That was great family fun.

Additionally, I remember going to San Francisco Giants baseball games with my various sons, first at Seals Stadium, then later at Candlestick Park. We would park on city streets and bring our own peanuts and sandwiches to save money.

When the kids were in their teen years, one thing I never got used to was waiting for them to come home at night from the movies or parties. I didn't sleep a wink until I heard each of them come through the front door. So whether they were on time or not, I lost a lot of sleep; but that was just my nature.

FAMILY FUN

One of the occasions that I enjoyed the most with my family was vacation time. We travelled to many places by car. In the early years, before the kids were in their teens, we all squeezed into our station wagon and went every place together. We went on trips of various duration to Yosemite National Park, Lake Tahoe, Santa Cruz beach, Russian River, Monterey, Disneyland, Big Basin State Park, and the Sierra foothills. We also went on many outings in the San Francisco Bay Area such as Tilden Park, Golden Gate Park, and Marin County. Some of our favorite , vacation spots were the P.G.&E. recreation camps that were available to employees in various parts of the state. We went to many of these as the weekly rates were very affordable.

In later years, some of the children went on vacation trips with Alicia and I as far away as the Pacific Northwest, Canada, Yellowstone National Park, Utah, and Nevada. Not all the children went on these trips because some had other committments. I remember that Richard occasionally couldn't get away because he couldn't find a substitute person for his paper route. Also, my older offspring had summer jobs, so they couldn't join us.

I have many happy remembrances about our family outings. It would take me a long time to write in detail about them. The following are just examples of events still vivid in my mind:

The vacation camping trip with Michael and Teresa along the Oregon Coast and then river rafting down the

Rogue River; the camping trip in Yosemite, where Michael and Richard almost got trampled by a huge black bear as they were in their sleeping bags; the many vacations in Lake Tahoe where we rented a house for a week and where everyone had fun out in the wilderness. Gavina, the kids' grandmother, and Paul Arias my nephew, were with us on some of these trips and we enjoyed their company a lot.

I also went swimming and fishing at the P.G.& E. Pit River Camps with Jess and Albert; I was never much of a fisherman so we never caught anything. We went on a trip to Mexico City and Acapulco with Gloria and Teresa where we got stuck in an elevator in a Mexico City hotel. We took a trip with the family to Lake Almanor and my boyhood town of Westwood. No one seemed too impressed with the height of the hills where I had risked my neck as a youngster riding down the hill in a sled. I tried to convince them that the passing years must have somehow levelled down that hill.

A lot of our outings were short one day trips. This was because we couldn't afford to stay overnite anywhere in a motel. So we would all pile into our station wagon at the crack of dawn and head out for Yosemite or Clear Lake or wherever we were going. After a days fun we would then head for home and usually arrived very late at night. Well needless to say, the children had fun at our destination but they hated the long hot drives. During those drives I often wondered whether it was worth it, what with all the complaints, noise, and frequent restroom stops.

Another pastime that I should mention were the frequent trips to San Jose where my brother, Ray, and his family lived. Our children got along real good with their cousins Corrine, Marty, Norma, Ellen, Joey, and Jo Ann

Herrera. An especially fond memory of mine in the early days were the visits to their small rented house in the middle of a fruit orchard on Lawrence Road. We all played badminton across the backyard fence, and we picked all the fresh delicious ripened fruit that we could eat. At times Ray and I would sneak away from everyone and go play golf at a nearby par three short course. That was my introduction to golf and to this day I thoroughly enjoy the game.

HOLIDAYS AND SPECIAL DAYS

Christmas and Thanksgiving have always been special festive days in our home. The boys used to help me put up outdoor Christmas lights on the house, and Alicia and the girls would do most of the tree decorating. For Christmas as an economy measure we had a plastic tree about five feet tall which we put up for many years. The tree would have to be assembled branch by branch. We finally discarded it because some branches were missing and everyone got tired of it. Later on we got trees from a lot or else cut them fresh at a tree farm. Most of the time we opened presents on Christmas morning, but as time went by the kids talked Alicia and I into opening presents on Christmas eve. Of course, going to Christmas Mass together as a family was our tradition especially in the early years. Also for many years we would take the family to San Jose where we would spend Christmas day visiting with Ray my brother, and his family.

For Christmas I always tried to give Alicia a very special card and gifts. Lingerie, perfume, and jewelry was what I customarily wound up giving her. Gloria and Teresa would sometimes do the wrapping for me since they could do a better job at this than I. Alicia seemed to like these presents and over the years I must say that she has accumulated a good collection; especially of jewelry.

On Thanksgiving Day the San Jose Herreras and other relatives would come to our house to have a sumptuous dinner put on by Alicia. The guests also included Alicia's mother Gavina, Alicia's sister Rita and her husband Henry, Paul and Laura Arias (Rita's children), Isobel, my sister and her husband Vidal, and their two sons David and Phillip Estrada, and Toni, my sister and her husband Bill Tryforos. We always had a home cooked turkey and ham with all the traditional trimmings. The aroma of all the delicious food being cooked filled the house from early morning. We never had enough space at our dining room table for everyone to sit there, so some of the younger kids had to sit at another table in the breakfast room. It's a good thing that we had a large house because all day long kids were running about, and noisely playing games, visiting with their cousins, and having fun.

Besides the above, our home has been the scene of many happy celebrations. Baptisms, confirmations, weddings, graduations, anniversaries, birthdays, reunions, holidays, and get-togethers have all been occasions for family celebrations. Each one of these events has been a special one honoring a particular event, or member of the family at various stages of their lives. I will not describe them here because I cannot do justice to them all.

Over the years I've also enjoyed the occasions when we've gotten together with our other young relatives who live out of our area. This has included Sam and Francis Garcia's children, Sammy, Becky, Gregory, and Priscilla, and my sister Janie's two boys, Bobby and Danny Alonzo. Our family has participated in activities with these folks at various times, but again I will not give details here because of my self-imposed limitations.

MY CHILDREN AS ADULTS

By year end 1979, my children were all grown up. In fact my two oldest boys, Jess and Albert, were married. Albert was married in Davis, California in 1973 to a veterinary student named Peggy Alpert, and Jess was married in Scotland in 1978 to a young lady named Martha Helen Kerr. I now had two daughters-in-law whom I learned to love dearly. Gloria had graduated from college and was living close by, but away from home. Michael was away at college. Richard and Teresa, our two youngest, were going to nearby colleges and still lived at home.

I really appreciated the fact that Richard and Teresa were still constantly around me at home. Their presence made the transition of having fewer people about the house easier for me. After all, I had been used to a large family at home for a long time. Also in these later years, the main burden of helping me around the house fell on Richard and Teresa even though they were busy with their own lives. I remember incidents like Richard helping me solder copper water pipes in the basement, and the times when he held me by the legs to prevent me from falling as I leaned out the upstairs windows painting. Teresa helped me pull wires through electrical conduit and also helped with car repairs and oil changes. It seemed like I was constantly doing maintenance either on the house or on the car.

Nevertheless, by that time in my life I had to get used to the fact that my children were all adults and in fact running their own lives. At times that was not easy for me, as in a few instances their decisions were not what I would have done. But in general I honestly tried to respect their positions, realizing that time brought constant changes into all our lives. Also, I had a lot of confidence in their judgement, so at no time was I really upset or worried about their directions in life. They knew that I was still there to provide help and counsel if they wanted it. The happiness of each individual in my family has always been very important to me.

9
The Later Years

WORK ACTIVITIES - EARLY 1980'S

As Chief Electrical Engineer for Pacific Gas & Electric Company (P.G.&E.), I had a large office on the 24th floor of the main headquarters building at 77 Beale Street in San Francisco. My office faced easterly so I had a magnificent view of San Francisco Bay and the East Bay hills. I felt very fortunate to have such pleasant working quarters. I soon got into a habit that whenever I needed to reflect on a problem, I would sit in my large swivel chair and gaze out at the sailboats in the bay, or else look at the reflection of the sun upon the far-away hills; this was very relaxing and stimulating. Also, for the first time since I had been employed I had a private secretary. Her name was Nancy Davido and we developed a professional friendship right away. She was knowledgeable about office matters, and she encouraged me to dictate my letters and memorandums. I soon got quite good at this.

Now that I was the Chief Electrical Engineer, I immediately found out that it was a very demanding job with long hours of work and much responsibility. I expected this of course, but it took me quite a while to learn how to approach my new job because it had both technical and managerial functions.

The technical content of the department's electrical engineering output was, in the final analysis, my responsibility. The Company relied on my department's expertise in all electrical generation, transmission, and distribution work. They expected the work to be done on time, within financial budgets, to be operationally sound and safe, and to comply with all codes and standards. My Professional Engineer Stamp or signature was affixed to every drawing and specification made in the department. Also, as the Chief Electrical Engineer, it was I that had to set the direction and make the major and tough technical decisions. Nevertheless, this technical part of the job was just a natural extension over what had been my past experience, and so I felt comfortable in this new role.

However, the managerial aspects of the position were for the most part a newer experience for me. I had full management control of the 140 persons in the department. Most were professional engineers. I had the final say on salaries and all personnel matters. So it turned out that much of my time was spent on administrative matters. My boss, Don Brand, the Vice President of Engineering, also was new in his position. So I not only had to run my department, but also had to meet frequently with Don and give him reports and counsel. I had to provide him with support as questions came up from the top management of the Company or from outside agencies. Don Brand and I developed a mutual respect and friendship during the next ten years.

I was attracted to the formal principles of management during my Santa Clara University days, when I had taken several management type courses in the School of Business. I found out that it takes more than good common sense, knowledge of the business, and a suitable personality to be a good manager; there is a process and discipline that is required in order to supplement one's natural management style. So at P.G.& E., in order to have everyone working together, several of my key supervisors and I took Company sponsored management training courses. I was determined to run my department with a much more business orientation than what had existed before. However, I found out that engineers did not readily see the need for the formalization of their work. They were set in their ways and making the changes I wanted was not easy. Nevertheless, I persevered and we made much progress together as time went by. After about three years, by 1983, my department was the best run department of all the engineering discipline departments, according to certain Company sources.

One of the things I took an avid interest in was the recruitment of young engineers into the department. The Personnel Department of the Company was responsible for the recruitment of engineers. But I soon found out that this was not working for me. Neither the quality nor the number of potential hires for our department were to my liking. So I embarked on a recruiting program wherein a few of our good young engineers would go out to targeted universities and do the initial screening for potential hires. We established good working relationships with the college engineering professors and thus we were able to talk to their bright students. A few of the graduating students were then invited to San Francisco for final interviews. My key supervisors and I did the final interviewing, and the best candidates were then offered entry level jobs in our organization. The recruitment program was a success and this model was eventually used throughout the General Office departments for recruiting new technically trained personnel.

Once on board, I took a lot of interest in the training and development of those young engineers. They were given specific rotational assignments, attended special seminars, and worked under a senior mentor engineer who was responsible for their work and development. The word soon got around at the universities that the P.G.& E. Electrical Engineering department was a good place to work. This made my job easier in recruiting new engineers at a time when there was a shortage of engineering graduates with an interest in electrical power.

One of the most difficult events that the Company went through during the 1980's was the re-analysis of all the design that had been done to date at the Diablo Canyon Nuclear Plant. The complete plant design had to be reviewed and the results documented. Also newer standards of design were required to be integrated into the plant. This was a very extensive process and one which eventually took about six years to complete. It affected all disciplines of engineering and construction. I, of course had to coordinate this effort for my department and it took up a lot of my time. I attended countless design review meetings, met with staff and management, and attended Nuclear Regulatory Committee meetings in San Francisco and Washington D.C.

This review was vital to me because I was the person who had done the basic engineering for many of the electrical systems in the plant including the generator, main transformers, and switchyard. As it finally turned out, the Electrical Engineering function passed the reviews in good shape. We had designed the components and systems with enough margin, so that only relatively few modifications were necessary on the electrical systems. I was very happy and proud that we had done a good job from the very beginning on this plant.

INDUSTRY COMMITTEE INVOLVEMENT

An aspect of my job that I really liked and appreciated was my involvement in various electric industry committees. As Chief Electrical Engineer, part of my job was to represent the Company on committees that set standards for the utility industry. So during the 1980's, I attended many conferences, seminars, and a few conventions. These meetings were held in various parts of the country and so this required travel on Company business averaging about one week every two or three months. From the very beginning I made a decision to take Alicia with me on these trips whenever we could. This worked out well since the children were all grown up by then, and also we could afford the extra expense. On these business trips the Company reimbursed me for most of my expenses, but we paid for all of Alicia's expenses.

The Appendix gives a listing of the various committees, and technical and professional societies that I belonged to. Additionally, it lists some industry-university relationships that I have been involved with. This university contact and advisory work has been a long time effort of mine to encourage engineering education among young people, especially minorities. As of this writing I am still active in this volunteer work.

As a result of this committee involvement, I have travelled and visited many cities in all parts of the continental U.S., as well as in Hawaii, Canada, Mexico, and several countries in Europe. This experience has been very broadening and I thoroughly enjoyed meeting other industry people. The electrical industry people that I met were all very nice almost without exception. Since P.G.& E. is a large utility and a leader in the industry, my attendance at the meetings and conferences seemed to give me a special status among my peers from other utility companies. My input was always solicited and listened to with respect at those meetings.

Whenever I had a chance I took an extra day or two on my own for sightseeing in the various localities. As a result I have seen many interesting museums, churches, monuments, buildings, parks, and historical landmarks. Washington D.C. is my favorite tourist city in the U.S.A.; here I have visited the remarkable Smithsonian Museum, the beautiful Catholic Basilica of the Immaculate Conception, the imposing Washington, Lincoln, and Jefferson Memorials, the elegant White House, the somber Arlington Cemetery, and many other marvelous sights in our nation's capital.

FOREIGN TRAVEL

Every two years in Paris, France there is an International Conference on Large High Voltage Electric Systems. This is a very prestigious technical meeting of electrical engineering experts from all over the world. During the 1980's I represented the Company as a member of this organization and so I have been fortunate enough to attend four of these conferences. It was an opportunity of a lifetime to go to Paris and Europe. Paris is absolutely the most impressive city that I have been to. It is unique. Its boulevards, buildings, museums, parks, sidewalk cafes, people, cathedrals, waterways, and monuments are all fabulous in my estimation. If anyone reading this ever goes to Europe, don't miss Paris.

Each time I went abroad Alicia went with me as I dared not even suggest that she stay at home. Even though it was expensive for us, we wanted to take advantage of the opportunity. On every occasion we always took a vacation so that we could see different countries and cultures. As a result we have been to many places in France, Scotland including Edinburgh, London, Italy including Venice, Florence and Rome, many cities in Spain and Portugal including Madrid and Lisbon, Germany including Berlin, and a trip through the Alps countries including Swiss and Austrian cities like Zurich, Geneva, Munich, and Vienna.

We thoroughly enjoyed all these localities, but for me the highlight of all these trips was seeing Pope John Paul II in person and close up, at the magnificent St. Peter's Square in Rome, in September, 1982. I'll forever remember the Pope's magnetic and Holy presence as he passed only a few yards away in his "Popemobile," giving Alicia and I and thousands of others, his blessing.

Another indelible remembrance was being at the Berlin Wall. Alicia and I were at "Checkpoint Charlie", the border crossing between West and East Berlin. As we stood on an elevated platform and looked towards East Berlin I could see beyond the Wall. There was barbed wire, then a 50 yard clearing (probably mined), armed patrol guards with leashed dogs, two high towers with protruding machine guns, and guards peering toward the West with binoculars. What a sight. All this was not to keep people from coming into East Berlin, it was the opposite, i.e. to prevent their people from fleeing to a freer life in the West. None of us should ever take our freedom here in the good old U.S.A. for granted. Fortunately, "The Wall" came down in 1990.

I could relate many more interesting and memorable trips and travel sights, but this is not a travelogue. But I did want to bring out the fact that my position in the Company during the 1980's gave me a unique opportunity to travel and mingle with people of different viewpoints and cultures.

As head of the department, I had control over many people so I had to be more aware of their problems, hopes, and aspirations. As a result I tried to become much more people oriented. I believe that my travel exposure made me a much better manager and a better person, and made me more considerate of those less fortunate than I.

At the same time, my experience as Chief Electrical Engineer made me more thankful to the Lord for making my life such a full one. This experience has strengthened my view, that only through education, hard work, understanding of human nature, and support by family, will young people of Mexican-American heritage be able to carve out a decent place for themselves and any offspring, in this country. So far it's worked for me, and my prayer is that these principles also work for all my descendants.

FAMILY GROWN UP

Concentration on my career and travelling with Alicia to various places was facilitated by the fact that my family was essentially away from home by the mid-1980's. Michael and Richard had finished college and were married. Michael was married in San Jose, California in 1983 to a girl named Gail Linda Garber, and Richard was married in 1985 in San Francisco to a young lady named Suzi Marcia Serna. Both of these fine women are very dear to my heart. Gloria was not married but was working hard at her career. Teresa was away from home at college and working towards getting her B.S. degree in Civil Engineering. As mentioned before, Jess and Albert were by now happily married, and starting to raise a family of their own.

As a result Alicia and I were alone at home for the first time since our marriage. What an eerie feeling. There was no radio playing loudly nor constantly, the phone didn't ring very often, the bathrooms were always available, our food bill went down drastically, young people didn't wander in and out of the house, and I got more sleep. However because everyone did not leave the nest and go out on their own at once, I adjusted quite well to this new phase of my life. A big change was that financially we were essentially through with educational and living expenses for our children. With the Lord's help we had passed those financial hurdles.

Obviously I missed the companionship of having the children around, but at the same time this gave Alicia and I an opportunity to rediscover each other, so to speak. We had a new found freedom. It gave us a chance to do more things together once again; things that we enjoyed doing like going out to dinner, and travelling. Alicia was a great companion and wife, and supportive of all my activities. Also, to keep busy and do something different from raising a family, she worked for many years at Standard 5 & 10 Stores on California Street.

A very memorable event happened about this time in June, 1983. Our children and daughters-in-law got together and gave Alicia and I a surprise 35th wedding anniversary party. This took place at Jess (my son) and Helen's house in Fremont on a warm sunny day and the surprise element took my breath away. Many relatives and friends showed up and a special treat was the presence of folks from out of the area. These included Toni, my sister, and her husband Bill Tryforos from Palm Springs, Francis (Alicia's sister) and her husband Sam Garcia who came from Barstow, Al and Bernice Garber (Michael's in-laws) from Pacifica, and Janie, my sister, and her husband Juan Alonzo who came from El Paso, Texas. (Historical note: Janie passed away years later on February 25, 1989).

The people present, plus delicious food, lots of beer and wine, music, and a festive atmosphere all contributed to a wonderful day. We received several gifts including a beautifully put together picture album depicting our life as it had progressed through the years. Alicia and I were deeply touched by this outpouring of love from everyone present. We especially appreciated the efforts and thoughtfulness of our children and daughters-in-law.

By 1984, it was hard for me to realize that I was now 60 years old. How ancient! But with my family now grown, I looked forward to working hard for the next five years and then retiring from P.G.& E.

10
Vice President of General Construction

MY SUPER PROMOTION

I was conducting a supervisor's workshop one evening in late March, 1984 at a downtown hotel when I received a message to call George Maneatis, who was President of Pacific Gas & Electric Company. Even though I knew George well, I immediately wondered why he wanted to talk to me, especially this late in the day. My first thoughts were that something had gone wrong at Helms Powerhouse, which was a Project under construction and where we were having problems on some equipment that I was responsible for. However, the subject of the subsequent phone conversation was totally unexpected and beyond my wildest dreams. He wanted to know if I would accept a position as an officer of the Company. The job he was talking about was Vice President of General Construction. Instinctively, and after catching my breath, I accepted.

So on March 21, 1984, the Board of Directors of Pacific Gas & Electric Company appointed me to the officer position of Vice President of General Construction.

This position had been vacant for a short time due to the illness and sudden death of the previous incumbent. The promotion was especially a surprise to me because I was not a career construction person; my background was in engineering. Of course I knew about the construction business because engineers and constructors had to work together on all projects. But all previous holders of this position were "hard hat" types with managerial experience in running large projects in the field. At this particular time many important and expensive major projects were under construction, and the financial stability of the Company depended on these projects being successfully completed. So it was a very gratifying affirmation by the Company Management, of my technical and managerial capabilities when they decided that I was the best man for the job. They selected me over several other candidates.

I must say however, that I had never pictured myself in such a high position in the Company. While I had no doubts in my abilities to cope with the challenges of the new position, it took me a long time to get over the euphoria of my promotion. Also, I should note here proudly, but with some degree of modesty, that at that time I was the highest ranking Hispanic employee in the Company and the first Mexican - American to reach Officer level in the history of P.G.&E.

My first action on the evening of my appointment, was to treat Alicia to a sumptious dinner celebration in a fancy restaurant on the top floor of the Bank of America building. We had wine and a wonderful dinner including dessert, along with a fabulous view. Alicia shared in my happiness and little did she know that for the next few years she also would be in the limelight at Company functions as the wife of an officer. Also, I immediately notified each of my children about my promotion because I knew that they too would feel a family pride in this achievement. They all were very happy and felt that the promotion was well deserved. Another thing I did was to give thanks to the Lord for this opportunity. I was convinced it was His will being done once again.

VICE PRESIDENT OF GENERAL CONSTRUCTION POSITION

As I have mentioned before, P.G.&.E is a very large Company with over 26,000 employees and is spread over a large geographical area in California. My new position was one of about 30 officer positions in the Company. Each officer headed up a major activity or geographical business entity. As Vice President of General Construction, I was the Corporate Officer responsible for providing the construction services needed to install and make operable plant and facilities for the Company. This included all forms of generation, transmission, and distribution of both electric and gas energy forms. My organization was the largest in the Company. It had about 4,200 Company employees. We were basically a field organization, with our work crews spread out all over the P.G.&E. territory. Only a relatively few General Construction folks were stationed in San Francisco. This included my office, those of my six department managers, and our support staffs.

My office was at 345 Mission Street which was across the street from the Company headquarters. On my first visit to the office I noticed that the office space was huge but the furnishings looked drab. I soon found out that as an officer I had a lot of power. All I had to do was ask and things would get done. So soon thereafter, the room was refurbished by a professional decorator, including new paint, and all new furnishings. It even had a closet with a wash basin and mirror. When the decorators were finished, the office still looked functional, but very nice. My immediate office staff consisted of an executive secretary named Melissa Lacombe, a typist-clerk, and an administrative engineer. These people turned out to be a big help to me because they knew all the office procedures and protocol.

I was assigned a brand new Company owned car that was mine to use on Company business and for commuting to and from work. Since I had to do a lot of travelling to visit the construction sites, I subsequently piled up a lot of mileage on this Chevrolet Caprice.

Although the construction forces were working on a multitude of both electric and gas projects, I spent most of my time following the progress and addressing problems on a few major jobs that were under construction. These projects were the Diablo Canyon Nuclear Plant, Helms Pumped Storage Hydro Plant, Geysers Geothermal Power Plant, and Kerckhoff Hydro Plant. These four facilities represented billions of dollars in construction expenditures, so the Company Management was vitally interested in their progress.

Every Monday morning there was a mandatory meeting of all Company officers. We gathered in the Board

Room of the Company headquarters building. At this meeting everyone would take turns and make presentations or give reports on their respective areas of responsibility to the Chief Executive Officer of the Company. I usually came through these briefings O.K., but whenever we had major problems on the projects mentioned above, my reports were not always well received. Ultimately however, these jobs were all successfully completed, and my contributions were recognized.

DEPARTMENT ACHIEVEMENTS

As Vice President of General Construction, I received very little direction from my boss, George Maneatis, President of the Company. This came about probably because he was doing other things and he had confidence in how I was handling the job. So besides making sure that the construction activities went well, I set my own goals for the Department. Upon arrival in my new job I found out that throughout the company General Construction (G.C.) was not looked upon very favorably. The various Operating Divisions and other General Office departments treated our folks like a "bunch of construction stiffs". As a result morale was quite low even among the professional and well educated technical staffs. I immediately set about to try to change this.

The first thing I did was to address the morale problem. I made several changes in our managerial ranks. As opportunities arose, I set aside people that were not willing to effect changes. I replaced them with hand picked people mostly from outside the Department in order to get some fresh ideas. I tried to encourage professionalism in our ranks by rewarding those who had, or obtained, business, construction, or engineering degrees. We recruited new engineers from universities using the model I had developed in my Electrical Engineering days. For the physical field personnel, I instituted several changes. We tried to treat each employee as a valuable Company resource. We increased their levels of training and made clear to them the criteria for promotion. We increased our efforts to give them more recognition when deserved. We wanted to make them feel like first class employees again.

For example, I was constantly out in the field at recognition and award luncheons. Whenever we had our Service Award Banquets I made sure that those affairs were at the best facility, with a good program, and with many Company officers in attendance to pay them homage. For the first time, employees' wives were invited to those banquets. On those nights we also paid for the service award recipient's hotel room so that they would not have to drive long distances back to their home areas that night. This type of treatment for General Construction employees was unheard of previously.

During the next several years I also instituted many major changes in how we went about our work. Chief among these were several innovative productivity improvements that saved the Company millions of dollars every year. These were not only physical work force related improvements, but also included field office computerization of many clerical functions. We also consolidated offices, negotiated innovative contracts with contractors, and finished many major projects ahead of schedule and under budget. Additionally, our safety record started to improve dramatically due to a campaign I instituted. The number of disabling injuries and accidents among our workers was reduced drastically.

G.C. was soon the Company leader in savings under the Suggestion Plan. Additionally in 1987, one of my Departments won the Chairman's Award for the most outstanding department in the whole Company.

The Management was starting to notice that G.C. was a dynamic organization second to none in the Company. More importantly the G.C. employees were happy to be part of this organization and morale was improving. Our employees' productivity was improving, and for the first time we were attracting top people as transfers from other parts of the Company. General Construction was on the move. As a result, I received many plaudits from my bosses, peers, and subordinates. I was glad that some of my goals were being achieved. However, I knew that most of the credit belonged to my employees. All I did was to provide leadership so that G.C. could succeed. During my five years as Vice President of General Construction I was very loyal to my employees and I respected each of them, no matter whether they were an apprentice field hand or a department manager.

COMPANY FUNCTIONS

Another one of my unwritten duties as a P.G.&E. Vice President was to represent the Company at a multitude of civic, social, business, and educational functions. These included fund raising events for charitable causes like United Way and the Boy Scouts, award banquets of all types, luncheons and meetings with business, civic, and educational leaders, and industry conferences. Including internal Company functions, I attended about three of these events every week for many years. Many of these events were held at night and in various localities, but mostly in California. At the formal functions more often than not, I was expected to say a few words or in some cases deliver a speech. In many instances I was the keynote speaker or the Master of Ceremonies. So out of necessity, I learned to be a pretty fair speaker.

Another unwritten rule was that Alicia was expected to join me at most of these events. However, she enjoyed being in the limelight and always accompanied me when appropriate. Alicia always made a good impression on all the dignitaries we met; I think because of her class, poise, sincerity and beauty. She was especially a favorite with the other Officers' wives. I always enjoyed having her along because it made me feel more at ease, and I was very proud of her presence besides me.

P.G.&E. had a couple of Company airplanes during the late 1980's that were used to carry executives and other employees to projects and localities where, or when, it was not convenient to fly commercial. I flew on the Company plane many times to various projects in our service territory. But I also used the Company plane on many Company functionary trips to places like Eureka, Fresno, Red Bluff, and Sacramento. Many of these trips were taken in the evening after normal work hours because of my busy work schedule. I'll never forget the time that Alicia and I were the only passengers on the plane on a trip to San Diego. We flew down the Pacific Coast on a clear evening and saw all the sights along the way, including Monterey Bay and Catalina Island. Being a humble person, I never quite got used to the fact that whenever I needed it, the airplane was there waiting for me. But I must say that I enjoyed the privilege.

ROLE MODEL

The fact that I was a Mexican American in a high corporate position, drew the attention of ethnic minorities from within the community, at universities, and within the Company. I had numerous requests to appear at their various functions as a means of motivation for their constituents. They held me up as a role model of a person of humble beginnings "who had reached the top." Since I was cast into this spotlight by natural circumstances, I rarely turned down opportunities to appear before minority groups, especially Hispanics and Blacks. However, I took on this mantle only because I sincerely wanted to help others, and not to satisfy my own ego.

I especially enjoyed trying to motivate young people at colleges and universities throughout central California. As a result, I participated at many scholarship functions, at career symposiums, engineering seminars, and small group counseling sessions. At each one of these functions I tried to be as inspirational as I could. I tried not to preach to them but at the same time I tried to make them realize that it would take hard work, an education, and confidence in themselves, in order to be able to reach their potential. I gave them practical advice based on my experience in the working world. After every session, I in turn was refreshed by the enthusiasm and youthful eagerness of the students, both male and female. In fact, these events were a welcome change from the harsh give and take of my everyday job responsibilities.

At the community level, I still remember quite vividly an evening in Visalia, California in July, 1987 where a veteran's Hispanic group was having their Annual State Convention. I was invited to be on the podium representing the Company. Many dignitaries were there including Pete Wilson, who at that time was the U.S. Senator from California. When Alicia and I got to the auditorium I was surprised to find out that I was on the program as one of the main speakers. Panic set in, because I usually prepared my speeches with great care. Anyway, I ad libbed, and gave the veterans their salute and tribute as best I could. However, my main impression of that night was the pride that I felt because of the presence of five Hispanic Congressional Medal of Honor winners from past wars. One of them was from El Paso, Texas. The courage and bravery of those Mexican Americans reaffirmed my belief that my heritage is a strong one.

The Hispanic Employees Association of the Company was very active in promoting recognition and advancement for their members. They constantly sought out my advice and they considered me their unofficial mentor. I helped them get better organized and advised them about preparation and qualities needed for advancement within the Company. I especially enjoyed attending their social functions because Hispanics know how to have fun. At their events, the Mexican food was always delicious. They usually had Mariachi music before dinner, then Latin type music for dancing, after dinner. I made many friends throughout the Company from this organization, and they all appreciated the help I gave them in furthering the goals of their organization. I felt good whenever I heard that an Hispanic had been promoted, not because he was a minority but because he deserved it. This was my constant theme to them.

SOCIETY OF HISPANIC PROFESSIONAL ENGINEERS

The Society of Hispanic Professional Engineers (SHPE) is a national organization dedicated to the advancement of Hispanic Americans in the technical professions of science and engineering. It helps it's members by promoting higher education and professional development programs. It is the largest professional organization in the nation with over 6000 members. SHPE has 30 professional chapters and over 72 student chapters at various universities and colleges. I have been involved with this organization for many years at both the local and national level, because it helps and encourages Hispanic youths to obtain a technical education.

SHPE has honored me at the national level on two occasions. The first is a feature article in the Winter 1986 edition of their magazine "Hispanic Engineer". My picture is on the cover and the article is titled "Professional Profile: Jess R. Herrera, Vice President of General Construction for PG&E". The four page article tells about my background and career, and my philosophy on education and engineering, and what it takes to get ahead in the Corporate world. Subsequent to its publication, I heard from many people telling me how inspiring the article was to them. This is what I had hoped for when I granted the interview to the Editor-in-Chief.

At the SHPE Thirteenth Annual Awards Banquet July, 1987, in Los Angeles, I was awarded the "HISPANIC IN TECHNOLOGY AWARD" for 1987. It was awarded for my numerous technical contributions, particularly in the field of Electrical Power Engineering. I considered this a great honor to receive this most prestigious award from such a fine organization. The plaque I received is on "The

Wall" in our home dining room.

The above "Role Model" and "SHPE" stories are just some episodes pertaining to being in the spotlight as a role model for ethnic minorities. I took this role very seriously as I knew that many people were judging Hispanics and other minorities by how I conducted myself. However, at no time did I consider that I was "on trial"; I had come up the hard way and earned whatever I had achieved. I just wanted to lead by example and help others in any way I could. Those extracurricular activities took me away from my main job and thus put a large strain on my time. But I was determined to carry through and I enjoyed the relationships. To this day I remain committed to helping others especially in the field of education, church, and community involvement. It's my attempt to give back some of my talents and experience for the benefit of others, just as others in the past did for me.

MEXICO CITY EARTHQUAKE

Another episode that I would like to relate was the trip I took to Mexico City following the earthquake there in 1985. On September 19, 1985 a very destructive earthquake hit Mexico City. Many large buildings were destroyed, hundreds of people died, communications to the outside world was cut off, electricity was shut off, water mains were broken, and human suffering abounded. A few days later I headed a four man team from P.G.&E. that went to Mexico City. The purpose of the trip was basically a good will mission from P.G.&E. and its employees towards the Mexican people.

Our trip lasted for four days. During this time we met with many relief and service organizations, with energy officials, and representatives of the Mexican government. Our aim was to determine what help the Company could provide on an immediate basis. We were well received by the Mexican authorities as they appreciated our offer of help. We visited some of the worst hit areas, such as hospitals and highrise apartment buildings that were in complete ruins. Hundreds of people were still buried in the rubble even after 12 days and the human suffering was visible everywhere.

As I stood there near the fallen rubble, I saw scenes that forever will be etched in my memory. I could hear the sounds of anguish from people that stood nearby hoping that their loved ones could be rescued. I smelled the stench of death and dust in the air. I saw the laborious efforts made by ordinary citizens to rescue, literally by hand, the trapped and buried unfortunate ones. I could feel the somberness and tension all around me as the Mexican people were making heroic efforts to pull through this tragedy. Thankfully, rescue teams and emergency supplies were coming in from countries all over the world, including the United States.

As the result of this trip, I made recommendations to the Company on specific material, funds, and humanitarian needs that were later acted on for the benefit of the Mexican people. Our employees were greatly interested to hear about this trip and were appreciative of my efforts. I was glad that I had helped the land of my ancestors in their time of need.

JOB SELF-ASSESSMENT

By January, 1989, I had been Vice President of General Construction for almost five years. In looking back on what I had accomplished during this time, I felt that I had done a good job.

I had been thrust into a very difficult management position, and at a time when several major Company projects needed to get completed. These projects were all subsequently completed with the help of my contributions. Additionally, I had made improvements to a ponderous and drifting organization, and G.C. was now on the road to being a competitive and accepted organization within the Company.

I had instituted programs at all levels of the organization so that our personnel were better trained and ready for advancement. I'm proud of the fact that to date, three of my department managers, Bill Mazotti, Phil Damask, and Jim Pope have been promoted into Officer positions in the Company.

Furthermore, I felt that I had been a good spokesman for the Company, and a humanitarian to enhance the Company's image. The majority of these latter activities were undertaken because of my personal interest in people and not because of some mandate from the Company.

So all in all, I figure that the Company had gotten its money's worth out of me. I was now approaching the end of my working career and I must say that, with few exceptions, I was happy at how things had turned out for me.

11
Retirement

P.G.&E. CAREER ENDS

The Company has a rule for Officers requiring mandatory retirement from P.G.&E. at age 65. I reached this age in January, 1989 so my official retirement date was February 1, 1989. It was difficult for me to realize that after a 43 year career, I was now approaching retirement from work. I had been so busy, especially during the last ten years in positions of heavy responsibility, that time had just zoomed by. I had put most of my energies into my work and had never given retirement any serious thoughts.

However, as the date approached, I did start to think about what it would be like to not have to go to work. I knew that I consciously would not miss the work and pressure of the job, but I would miss the associations with the people whom I worked with. Also, I knew that by keeping up with family, home, hobbies, and other activities, I would be able to keep myself busy and not get bored; this was just my nature. Therefore, as my retirement date drew nearer, I resigned myself to the fact that retirement was imminent. In fact, since I was given no choice, I actually started to look forward toward retiring.

MY RETIREMENT PARTY

It was customary at P.G.&E. to give a person who was retiring some sort of a sendoff by his work associates. This usually took the form of a luncheon or a dinner. In my case, Alicia, and Melissa, my secretary, decided that the most appropriate function would be a gala banquet; nothing less would do. So they set about planning for the festivities. As the result, my associates and friends at work gave me a retirement party that many say is the best ever given for a retiree at P.G.&E. Whether this is the case or not, I can say that from my perspective it was super!

It was an evening dinner affair held in a large hall in Alameda, California, in late January, 1989, and attended by about 160 people. The people present included all members of my immediate family, work associates, Company officers, and friends from both within and outside the Company. To add to the festive air some of my Hispanic employee friends hired a small mariachi band to play before dinner. Speeches were given by those at the head table, including Jess, my son representing the family, and George Maneatis, President of P.G.&E. In addition, I also received verbal accolades from associates, representatives of the community and electric power industry, universities, and Hispanic employee and professional groups. Besides these tributes, I also received many gifts, some money, a scrapbook, and a great many cards and letters wishing me a happy retirement.

I was overwhelmed by the large turnout of friends. Needless to say, I was grateful for that retirement party and was deeply moved by the program and speeches. It was an evening that I will never forget and a perfect way to cap a long career. I gave a short "thank you" speech but it was hard for me to express how appreciative I was to all those present for such a wonderful evening.

Having my family there at the retirement party, to share in this tribute to me, was the best present I received. In attendance were Jess and Helen, Albert and Peggy, who had come up from Los Angeles, Gloria, my beautiful daughter, and her friend Casey McGuire, Michael and Gail, who had made the trip from Colorado, Richard and Suzi, and Teresa my other beautiful daughter, and her friend Phil Teresi. Alicia was beside me at the head table and in a place of honor. Of course having her there was something special, but no one could have kept her away, since she has always been my main supporter; besides it was her early involvement in the planning of this banquet that gave my associates the green light to proceed with the function.

During those same days, other individuals and smaller groups of associates and friends also treated me to retirement luncheons. Included in these was an official Company function attended by only all the Officers. These Officers were the folks that ran the Company and whom I had worked alongside for the past five years. Their gifts included a new set of golf clubs for me and a necklace with a diamond on it for my wife. I was certainly going to miss these fine folks.

FAMILY REVISITED - GRANDCHILDREN

By the time of this writing in the Fall of 1991, our family had grown and I had been blessed with seven grandchildren. Even though this is not a story about my family, I feel compelled to mention the grandchildren here because they are something special.

Jonathan, a boy age twelve, and Meredith, a girl age eleven, are Albert and Peggy's offspring. I love these two youngsters dearly. They are the oldest of the grandchildren, and smart as can be. Even though they live in Southern California, we manage to see each other at least two or three times a year. They spend some time with Alicia and I in San Francisco during summer vacations, and we certainly look forward to their visits with much anticipation. Also we make it a point to travel to their home in Rancho Palos Verdes at the slightest pretext.

Jess and Helen have one son named Paul. He is a smart, lovable boy, age six with a very infectious laughter. He and I get along real good because he is full of fun, attentive, and athletic. I just love the way he wraps himself around me whenever he gives me a hug.

Jason, a boy age six, and Nicole, a girl age four, are Mike and Gail's children. Since they live in Colorado I don't see them as often as I would like. But we still manage to get together with them during the summertime and most Christmas seasons. I enjoy conversing and playing with Jason because he has an imagination second to none. When I tell him stories he listens with wide eyed attention. Nicole is very athletic and a beautiful little girl with lots of curly hair, and she likes to eat.

Richard and Suzi have two pretty little girls: Lauren, age four, and Lindsey, almost two years of age. Since they live close by in San Rafael, I'm very fortunate and see them quite often. Lauren is a very self-sufficient young girl and a delight to have around. She is good company for me as we take our walks. Her middle name, Jessica, is named after me. Lindsey was born on my birthday, January 18th, so we have a lot in common already. It's amazing how alert she is and how fast she's developing in all respects.

Alicia and I really love these children and feel blessed in having them and seeing them grow. I know we spoil them and cater to their wants but we can't help ourselves; that's what grandparents do. At times I try to be firm with them, but it doesn't work. I'll leave the discipline to their parents. I try to spend as much time as I can with them, even though they wear me out, because I want them to remember me after I'm gone. Since they all have good, caring parents I'm confident that they will grow up to be responsible, God loving individuals. That and good health is my hope for them, and for any other future grandchildren that may be born.

PERSONAL PROFILE

A future generation may wonder what I was like personally. Physically I'm five feet, eleven inches tall, and weigh about 155 pounds. I was thin as a boy, and as an adult I'm of medium build. I have a brownish complexion typical of Mexican Americans and my eyes are dark brown, and my hair is black but thinning and getting grey fast. I have been fairly healthy all my life, thanks to God, but my eyesight is failing gradually due to a central vein occlusion that happened about five years ago.

I have always been fairly even tempered, but tend to get impatient easily. I believe that I am a tolerant person, mostly because of my upbringing. My hobbies and interests are many. I have always loved sports and participated in them as a youngster. I especially like baseball, golf, and football. In college I boxed and played lots of handball and some tennis.

Listening to music of all kinds, from classical to jazz, is a favorite pastime. I especially like swing era big band music, of which I have a large collection of records, cassette tapes, and compact discs. Additionally, I like to doodle on the piano with my own original slow blues and jazzy chordal themes. I like to keep busy fixing things around the house and working in the garden. The only movies I like are those involving adventure and intrigue. My favorite food is Alicia's enchiladas.

Trying to live up to the tenets of my Catholic faith has been a life-long endeavor.

LOOKING BACK

As I look back on my life to date, I have a sense of satisfaction and accomplishment. I have done the best I could in raising my family, in reaching high level positions in my chosen career, and in helping others. I learned about love for one's family from my parents. And despite the handicap of losing them at an early age, I persevered past a poor environment and discrimination to achieve a rewarding career.

I have been blessed with a wonderful family and a happy homelife. I have tried to have a positive influence in the lives of my children and of others by my example and encouragement. And I feel that my contributions via my career have indirectly made a difference in bettering the lives of people in California.

Besides my family, who has always supported me, I also owe thanks to many other persons who have helped me throughout my life. I haven't mentioned them all in this book but may God bless everyone of them. However, I feel very strongly that my constant companion has been the Lord. Whenever, the pressures got great and the obstacles high, God was always there. I needed only to ask for His help. I fervently hope that my descendants also benefit from God's goodness in the future.

Because a college education was my key to a better life, my personal crusade has been to reach out to young people to encourage them to get an education no matter what the odds are. Times have changed during my lifetime to the present very complex, competitive and worldwide economy. But times are still changing, and the quality of life, especially for younger people, can be strained as they cope to meet the the challenges of everyday living. It's my belief that only through the discipline of thinking, obtained via a higher education, will anyone have the opportunity for a better life for themselves and their children. For Mexican Americans in California all the more opportunity will exist, because some day they will be the majority population. And thus, the positions of leadership will be their responsibility as citizens of our great nation.

EPITAPH

People who read this story will form their own opinions about what I've done with my life. But what is important to me is that after I'm gone from this earth I hope that my loved ones say:

"He was a good husband, a good father, and a good grandfather."

ENDING

My life's story up to the time of my retirement from active work, is the end of this book. I have given the reader a glimpse of my past life. My future life is in the hands of God.

If He wills it, my personal plans for the immediate future include doing some professional consulting work, continuing to enjoy relationships with my wife, family, and grandchildren, travelling, continued involvement on university and community boards and on church councils, and working on special projects such as the writing of this book.

Additionally, I want to relax by playing golf, tending to my garden, doing some remodeling and maintenance on the house, engaging in a modest exercise program, becoming more proficient at playing the piano, learning more about finances and investments, and learning to use the personal computer that I bought with the money given to me by my friends at my retirement party.

Other than the above, in my spare time, I'll just sit on an easy chair on the deck that Richard made for us in the backyard, and read or sip a soft drink, or just think about nothing.

Photos

FATHER
ALBINO HERRERA
AGE 29   (1915)   AGE 18

MOTHER
SIMONA HERRERA

GRANDMOTHER
FRANCISCA RAMIREZ
AGE 58 - 1924

JESS   1941
BOWIE HIGH SCHOOL GRADUATE

TEXAS A&M COLLEGE - AGGIELAND ORCHESTRA - 1945
JESS FOURTH FROM LEFT FRONT

JESS IN SAN FRANCISCO - 1947

JESS & ALICIA - 1947
ENGAGED COUPLE

WEDDING PICTURE
JESS & ALICIA HERRERA - 1948

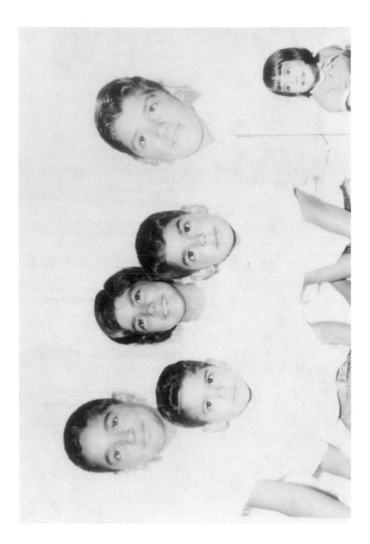

GROWING FAMILY - 1961 (L - R): ALBERT, RICHARD, GLORIA, MICHAEL, JESS JR., TERESA (1964)

JESS WITH SISTER,
ISOBEL ESTRADA - 1982

FAMILY HOUSE - 420 38th AVE
SAN FRANCISCO

SISTERS: JANIE ALONZO (L) &
TONI TRYFOROS - 1983

BROTHERS: JESS (L) & RAY
HERRERA - 1987

ALICIA HERRERA - 1986

JESS AT OFFICE - 1985

JESS GIVING A SPEECH - 1988

FAMILY - 1989

STANDING: (L - R)
        MICHAEL, GAIL, JESS, ALICIA,
        CASEY, GLORIA, JESS JR., HELEN,
        ALBERT, PEGGY

KNEELING: (L - R)
        RICHARD, SUZI, TERESA, PHIL

JESS WITH GRANDCHILDREN - 1988
(T - B): LAUREN,
JONATHAN, MEREDITH, PAUL

GRANDCHILDREN - 1990
(L - R): JASON, NICOLE, LINDSEY

HELMS POWERHOUSE - 1988
PACIFIC GAS & ELECTRIC CO.
(A Project Jess Worked On)

JESS IN PARIS - 1990

RETIRED: (Relaxing in Cancun, Mexico)

Appendix

My Life Chronology
Industry Committees and University Boards
Family Chart - Ancestors and Parents
Letter by Simona Herrera to her Brother
Letter by Juanita Herrera about her Father
History of Westwood, California

MY LIFE CHRONOLOGY
JESS ROBERT HERRERA

YEAR   IMPORTANT LIFE EVENTS

1918   Parents came to the United States from Mexico.

1924   Born on January 18, 1924 in Westwood (Lassen County), California.

1928   Father, Albino Herrera, died in June in Westwood.

1929-1935   Lived with mother and family in Westwood, and grew up during the Great Depression years.

1936   Mother, Simona (Ramirez) Herrera, died in March in Westwood, leaving me as an orphan. Went to El Paso, Texas with my grandmother. Lived with my sisters and brother in El Paso.

1937   Finished Junior High and started at Bowie High School in September. Entered into my teen years living in the slums (barrios) of South El Paso.

1938   Started taking music lessons.

1941   Graduated from Bowie High School in June. Played in a professional "Swing" orchestra. Got my first job as a "stock boy".

1942   Rejected for Armed Services duty during World War 2 for medical reasons. Started at Texas College of Mines in El Paso, taking engineering courses.

1944   Transferred to Texas A&M University at College Station, Texas. Paid for expenses by playing in the Aggieland Orchestra.

1946   Graduated from Texas A&M in May with a Bachelor of Science (BS) degree in Electrical Engineering. Relocated to San Francisco, California to live. Started work career at Pacific Electric Manufacturing Corporation as an electrical designer. Met future wife, Alicia E. Ramirez, in Oakland, California.

1947   Engaged to be married to Alicia.

1948   Married Alicia in San Francisco in June. Started married life in an apartment on Minnesota Street.

1949   Started a family; first son, Jess Alvino, born in April.

1950   Second son, Albert Anthony, born in October.

1951   Changed jobs. Started at Pacific Gas & Electric Company (P.G.&E.) in San Francisco, as a draftsman.

1952   Bought first home, on Farallones Street.

1954   Registered as a Professional Electrical Engineer in the State of California.

1955   First daughter, Gloria Alicia, born in January. Promoted to Engineering Department at P.G.&E.

1957 Michael Selso, a surviving twin son, born in March. The other twin son, Robert, died soon after birth.

1958 Family continues growing; Richard Ray, another son, born in February. Moved to a house at 420 38th Avenue in San Francisco. Celebrated our 10th wedding anniversary.

1961 Last child, Teresa Ann, a daughter, born in September.

1964 Promoted to Senior Electrical Engineer at work.

1965-1969 Continued in planning and design work at P.G.&E., working on many important substations, power plants, and transmission projects.

1970 Promoted to Supervising Electrical Engineer in the Electric Generation & Transmission Department.

1973 Celebrated our 25th wedding anniversary.

1974 Awarded a Master of Science (M.S.) in Engineering Degree from University of Santa Clara.

1976 Promoted to position of Assistant Chief Electrical Engineer.

1979 Appointed as Chief Electrical Engineer for P.G.&E. Children all grown by now; the three oldest had finished college, and the three youngest were finishing college.

1979-1983 Continued career as Chief Electrical Engineer.

1984   Appointed to Officer position at P.G.&E. as Vice President of General Construction.

1985-1988   Continued career as Vice President of General Construction. Involved in many high level Company activities.

1988   Celebrated our 40th weddding anniversary.

1989   Retired from P.G.&E. on February 1st after 37 ½ years with Company, and over 43 years after graduation from college.

COMMITTEE AFFILIATIONS
(Past and Present)
JESS R. HERRERA

UTILITY INDUSTRY

INSTITUTE OF ELECTRICAL AND ELECTRONIC ENGINEERS
Power Engineering Society
Power Education Committee

ELECTRIC POWER RESEARCH INSTITUTE
Electrical Systems Divisional Committee
Plant Electrical Systems and Equipment Task Force

EDISON ELECTRIC INSTITUTE
Construction Committee
Electrical Systems and Equipment Committee

PACIFIC GAS AND ELECTRIC
About 15 Internal Committees

INTERNATIONAL CONFERENCE ON HIGH VOLTAGE ELECTRICAL SYSTEMS

PACIFIC COAST ELECTRICAL ASSOCIATION

PACIFIC COAST GAS ASSOCIATION

UNIVERSITIES

SAN FRANCISCO STATE, DIVISION OF ENGINEERING
Advisory Board

SACRAMENTO STATE, DIVISION OF ENGINEERING
Electric Power Education Institute, Advisory Board

FRESNO STATE, SCHOOL OF ENGINEERING
Advisory Board

STANFORD, CONSTRUCTION EXECUTIVE PROGRAM
Steering Committee

CALIFORNIA POLYTECHNIC, SCHOOL OF ENGINEERING
Electric Power Institute, Advisory Board

OTHER

SOCIETY OF HISPANIC PROFESSIONAL ENGINEERS,
Member

ENGINEERS CLUB OF SAN FRANCISCO, Member

ELECTRIC CLUB OF SAN FRANCISCO, Member

COMMONWEALTH CLUB OF SAN FRANCISCO,
Member

BOY SCOUTS OF AMERICA
Construction Industry Steering Committee

SAN FRANCISCO RICHMOND DISTRICT NEIGHBORHOOD CENTER
Advisory Board

ST THOMAS APOSTLE CHURCH
Parish Council, Member

ANCESTRAL CHART

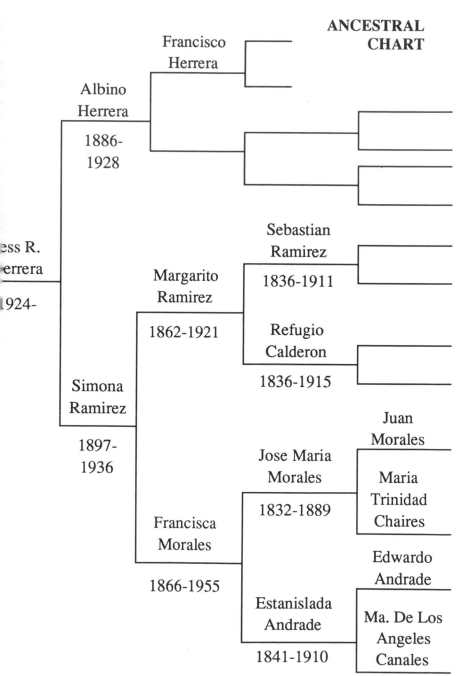

Francisco
Herrera

Albino
Herrera

1886-
1928

ess R.
errera

924-

Margarito
Ramirez

1862-1921

Sebastian
Ramirez

1836-1911

Refugio
Calderon

1836-1915

Simona
Ramirez

1897-
1936

Juan
Morales

Jose Maria
Morales

1832-1889

Maria
Trinidad
Chaires

Francisca
Morales

1866-1955

Edwardo
Andrade

Estanislada
Andrade

1841-1910

Ma. De Los
Angeles
Canales

TRANSLATION OF A LETTER WRITTEN IN SPANISH BY MY MOTHER SIMONA HERRERA, (AGE 33), IN WESTWOOD, CALIFORNIA ON DECEMBER 1, 1930, TO HER BROTHER FRANCISCO RAMIREZ (AGE 24) WHO LIVED IN EL PASO, TEXAS.

(The letter was written in ink. It was translated by Jess R. Herrera in December, 1989. The original of the letter was obtained from Janie Alonzo's (Simona's oldest daughter) papers upon her death in February, 1989).

Frisco:

    I am finally answering your letter that I received some time ago. Nevertheless, for me it was a very great joy that you would write to me because even though I know that my brother suffers naturally from a general weakening sickness, still I hope that he continues to write to me from time to time. Also I want you to be frank, sweet, and firm with me like united (close) brothers and sisters should be. What I don't like is that you consider yourself an embarrassment, because that does not result in anything with honor. Even if you believe that you have many vices, those in your blood family tend to be blind to reason, and love makes one forget all - right?

    Frisco, you should see how sad I am that you continue to be sick, but I trust in the Blessed Virgin of Carmel that She gives you your health, or at least a large amount of resignation and patience to suffer whatever God wants.

    Look Frisco, I wish that you do not ask more of

Jesus than to regain your health; ask with love that you be His servant and more united in His service because the more we ask of Him, the more He gives us what we need. You know that behind the hardships comes the penance and one should make a sacrifice of body and soul. To be able to understand this you don't know if another from your family has large failings. The generous God selects you to pay by means of your sickness and poverty. Notice that recently born and innocent babies also suffer serious illnesses and they owe nothing; except that they still pay for the errors of their parents and of sinners.

Note Frisco, that when you read about the lives of the Saints, many times their family members renounce them or do not believe in them. The week before last I read in a Catholic magazine that Saint Elodia, when she was left as a widow, was renounced by her three sons out of hypocrisy. They thought that with her personality she would dishonor them and they would not be able to endure the shame. So they asked that she leave them. As a result she suffered great pain because she had to leave her sons and because she was being despised by those she loved. She did not know what to do. She thought she could not serve God because nothing good was happening to her and at that moment she felt she did not have the right to ask God for sympathy or support. Nor did she want to offer Him a sacrifice because she feared that she would not complete her promises. This was because of her burdens today, and tomorrow might bring other pains and anxieties that she would have to bear until death.

But Saint Elodia knew that God does not burden anyone with things that human nature cannot bear up to. So because of her faith and confidence that she had at that moment, God appeared to her and said: "If you wish to save yourself I have three swords for your salvation of which you are to choose only one; they are sickness, slander, or persecution." Now Saint Elodia was glad to choose just one of these swords, but the angels who accompanied our Savior advised her not to choose one of her liking, but instead to leave the decision to His blessed will.

That was what she did, and at that moment the vision disappeared and she immediately began to feel the pains of the three swords that God had sent. But she found that the three swords combined were bearable and not as sharp as any one that she might have selected. She could not retire to a convent, but at least she did not die of hunger as she had feared she might. God proved to her that no one is born a saint, but what He wants is simply for one to submit to His will.

Now Frisco you should see that God has sent you your sickness and failing health, but you should give thanks that already many years (of good health) have gone by. We don't know if others with this same affliction have died within a short time. God gives strength to each of us up to the limits of our endurance, and if we, (together) with you, continue to ask for the salvation of your soul, I'm sure that you will get your just deserves. For this we should give thanks to God. Now (I know) this is difficult to bear because no one wants to suffer at all nor to feel bad, but it's only when one reflects on it a bit and has faith in God that we feel more at ease. And Frisco, you have the good fortune of having the Sacraments. Your Confessor can guide you in all your doubts. You should go frequently to receive the Bread of Life; in this don't be deterred.

Let mother have her way and don't disagree with

her in anything. We know her temperament and she has many faults, but you must let her convince herself about Manuel (Francisco's younger brother). You did right in placing him in the public school, maybe there they will be firmer with him. You did right because (schooling) is a necessity if he wants to ever earn a little money. He should do it because he knows that you can't give him any money. Furthermore, he is grown up now and what he needs is some learning. This should take place now that he is not a bad person. If he doesn't, then later on he will regret that he did not learn to read or write so that he can earn a living.

I have already told you to put him (Manuel) in school because that newspaper job has him on the streets all day. You can't deny that this allows him to come across bad friends and vagrants everywhere. I wish that since he is not interested in school, or because that's the way he is, you would make an effort for him to learn a trade. I wish he could find a job where he would be an understudy to someone; even if they didn't pay him well they could compensate him according to his application to the work.

Sometimes one accomplishes more when he is poor than when he has means and spends recklessly on things such as drugs. This does not result in anything good. First one must attend to obtaining food to eat and for other necessities. A refrain in Spanish says "aste sordo y te pondras gordo". (Literally this translates to: "be deaf and you'll get fat", but in context it probably means "turn a deaf ear to evil and you'll prosper").

It's a pity that one has to endure suffering and shame; but one has to offer all to the infant Jesus for the coldness that we endure. Look, I think this year many people are sad and poor like us upon waiting for Christmas. They cannot give anything (gifts) nowadays like in other years. No person has escaped this economic crisis and here everyone laments because with the very low wages they cannot buy things as they did before; many others do not even have a job. Juan, Arturo, Enrique, and several other men are all without work.

You know that some women are going to have even sadder days than in other years because on the feast day of the "Lupes" they are going to be in mourning. On my comadre (of Juanita) Leona's Saint's day, Don Mersed's father is dying and the poor man has been in Susanville for three days now. All his children are in deep sorrow and we commend him to the mercy of God as this man is in his last moments. Don't forget Frisco to send your condolences in a letter to Don Mersed. You know that the Perez and Gonzalez families are quite large and my comadre has relatives and many friends here in Westwood. My comadre's family is presently in Susanville but she will not go there until tomorrow when Chava does not work.

I am going to let Tonia and Juanita go with them in my place to pay our respects, because let me tell you that twelve days ago I dropped a pot of boiling water on my feet. Only one foot developed blisters and I walked for two days; but this exertion was bad for me and my foot got swollen and then I couldn't walk at all. Juanita had to stay home from school to help me so that the other children could go to school. Nothing else was wrong with my health but I had to keep my foot and leg extended. Leona acted like a sister to me. With her help I was cured soon and I am now walking around. But I still do not go out, nor does Leona let me, nor do I put on a shoe with a heel. I would look very funny in the midst of a lot of people in my house slippers. But I am well now thanks to God.

Frisco, ask my mother how she liked the little dresses that I made and sent to her the past week. Also I received the earrings she sent me and they look good. However, don't bother to repair the other earrings because they charge too much and it's not worth it.

You know Frisco, I'm going to send Manuel some calendars to see if he can help me by selling them from your house. Maybe he can profit some. You should encourage him to try. Maybe God will help him to have an interest in this. The money will be his (to keep) but don't tell him until I see how this goes.

Frisco, regarding Juanita and Tonia, they are well, but I sense that Juanita worries more than before because her school load is heavier now. She didn't use to bring work home but now she works on her class lessons every night. She is studying hard because everyone tells her that the first year is harder than the second. She is taking a college curriculum and I am in accord with this. Who knows maybe God will help her and she can finish these studies and get more from them than taking a general high school course of study. They advise her that it is better to take preparatory courses for college from the start rather than taking commercial courses. If she can she will go to college when she finishes, but if not, then she can get any job. Trini Gonzalez had already taken this course this past year but since she did not get suitable grades in a civics class, she had to take a commercial course this present year.

Hopefully, God will help us because Juanita only needs four more years to finish school and I am thinking of staying in Westwood only that long. If she can go to college then she can get a job in some other place - right? Then Tonia could finish high school elsewhere. In the end God will determine what He wants, and I hope that He continues to help us.

Frisco, ask the Blessed Virgin that She grant me a (special) favor that I need very much. She knows what worries me, and don't cease to ask Her because on this favor depends the well being of all my children. I don't want grand things for them, but only for them and I to be happy, in whatever manner God wants us to be, and without pretensions.

Look, in another letter I will tell (you) many more things. I hope I don't catch any disease such as yours so that I can take pencil in hand. Say hello to mother and to Maria (sister) and to the other "Maria la Presidenta".

Without further (words), your sister who does not forget you. Goodbye Frisco.

(signed)
S.R. Herrera

TRANSLATION OF A LETTER WRITTEN IN SPANISH BY JUANITA HERRERA IN WESTWOOD, CALIFORNIA DURING THE SUMMER OF 1928 CONCERNING THE DEATH OF HER FATHER, ALBINO HERRERA.

(The letter was written in ink. Juanita was 12-1/2 years of age at the time. The letter was translated by J. R. Herrera in December, 1989. The original letter was obtained from Juanita Alonzo's papers upon her death in February, 1989).

On the 5th day of June, 1928 our suffering started. On Tuesday the 5th at nine o'clock at night my mother (Simona) started to get sick from severe head and neck pain attacks which lasted from five to ten minutes each. She eventually lost consciousness and the last rites and Holy Sacraments were prayed over her. They took her to the hospital in Susanville where she was kept for four days. Quica (Juanita's grandmother), arrived on the 14th from El Paso. They then brought mother back to Westwood as she was then feeling better.

Two days later my father died on Saturday June 16, 1928 at three o'clock in the afternoon at the age of 42 years. He left 5 children and my mother: my mother who was 31 years of age, the oldest daughter Juanita, who was 12 years of age, Tonia of 10 years of age, Chuy (Jess) 4 years of age, Rey (Raymond) at 3 years, and Amalia at 5 months of age.

My father had been sick with influenza since April 17, 1928 and on the 8th day of June he got pneumonia. At seven o'clock at night (on the 15th) he developed blood hemorrhages which lasted until he died.

He was buried on the 18th day of June at 2:30 o'clock in the afternoon in Westwood cemetery with Father McCarthy doing the funeral. Many of his friends who loved him attended.

These lines are written so that I can have more stately rememberances of my adorable father.

Your very grief filled daughter
(signed) Juanita Herrera

(Footnote): My little sister Amalia died on the 30th of November, 1928 at the age of 10 months. She was buried alongside my father on December 2, 1928.

HISTORY OF WESTWOOD (LASSEN COUNTY), CALIFORNIA

FOREST LANDS

The town of Westwood, California in Lassen County, is in the Northeastern part of the state. It was founded by a very wealthy entreprenuer named Thomas Barlow Walker, who was born in 1840. T.B. Walker acquired his wealth in Minnesota as a lumber baron with vast timberland holdings there. By 1890, he and his partners were involved in large logging and mill operations, along with railroad and waterway connections that allowed them to cut, extract and transport millions of trees to his lumber mills. By 1890 the vast acreages of timber in Northern Minnesota were all logged out and he decided that California would be the next location for his Red River Lumber Company.

Walker liquidated most of his Minnesota holdings and started to purchase vast timberlands in Northeastern California. Basically he bought lands that were in remote sparsely populated areas, but rich in timberlands. Also, he was able to get these lands at bargain rates because, despite the timber, the land had very little value. This was because the holdings were inaccessible; there were no roads, no streams, and no railroads to the various sites. Even today this area of California is basically a vast empty wilderness with only a few small towns of any size. Walker's belief was that, despite the fact that his timber was far removed from large markets of any consequence, he could make these large virgin stands of trees pay off for him. He did exactly that and the Westwood Red River Lumber Company operations subsequently turned out to be a huge success. It also made him one of the wealthiest persons in the world.

The California land aquisition continued until 1913; by this time the Walker family owned outright, or in partnership, over a million and a quarter acres of prime timberland.

Walker set up his first base of operation in Northeastern California in the pioneer village of Susanville. Susanville is on the edge of the Great Basin, a largely arid semi-desert to the east. To the the west is the country where the northern end of the Sierra Nevada and the southern extremes of the Cascade mountains meet. These two ranges provide terrain in this area that is irregular and full of small valleys and gentle slopes with favorable climatic conditions that allow trees to grow in lush forests. There are no redwood trees in this area, but at that time pine trees grew in profusion and to majestic sizes. Additionally there were stands of fir and western cedar trees.

By 1910, T.B.Walker was ready to move on his dream of a western lumber empire. With guarantees of large lumber shipments, the Western Pacific (WP) and Southern Pacific (SP) Railroads completed construction of their rails; WP in 1909 from the south, to Susanville; and SP in 1914 from Fernely, Nevada to a location about 40 miles west of Susanville to a lumber camp named Westwood.

Susanville actively promoted their town to be the permanent site for the Red River mill and operations. However Westwood was chosen primarily because of contracts with the SP Railroad, and because a suitable large site was available for a mill pond that could be supplied with water from a ditch. Additionally, adequate space was available nearby for the planned lumber mill and town facilities.

WESTWOOD BORN

The very first tree cut by Red River in California was in September, 1912. Westwood's birthdate was about in 1912. It was a planned company town that was to profit from the Walker's earlier lumber town experience in Minnesota. Construction was planned in three phases. The first was a small portable mill made by hooking up a threshing machine to a circular saw on log skids. The lumber cut by this saw was used to construct a large and modern plant called "Mill B". When this mill became operational, its output was used to build a huge permanent installation called "Mill A", as well as buildings and houses for the town itself. All the machinery installed in the mills was of the latest modern technology, and of special design. The machines were designed to be driven mostly by electricity, as The Great Western Power Company was building a large hydro-electric development project nearby in the area.

By mid-summer 1913, the town was taking shape. A small group of buildings eventually called "Old Town" were the first small houses to be built. This area was actually part of a construction camp. Right next to Old Town was a man-made 320 acre mill pond. This water pond was fed by a ditch that originated about four miles to the east from a reservoir that was made by damming a small river named Robbers Creek. The mill pond was quite vital to the lumber operations as the logs were dumped here prior to processing.

This first settlement of Old Town was actually a ghetto for the construction workers. Most of these workers were of foreign nationalities such as Greek, Mexican,

Italian, Spanish, and Native Indians. These people were drawn and recruited from all parts of the country to this area to find work. The turnover of this labor force was was quite high. This was because the living conditions were harsh and at times primitive; one had to be tough and in excellent health to be able to withstand the rigors of the snow and cold of the severe winters. Nevertheless, these persons and families of foreign ancestry came to find work and full of hope to seek a better life than where they came from. For these early settlers it was a place where the the most humble and unskilled laboring class of people could find work and make a living for themselves. Although no official segregation was apparently intended, nevertheless it occurred for these people, as Old Town was basically a slum area.

COMPANY TOWN

Soon therafter, a newer set of houses and buildings were erected across from Robbers Creek and the mill pond. This emerging and more carefully planned area in Westwood was built up from the lumber output of Mills A and B. Also, a foot-bridge was built connecting Old Town to the mill and the newer town of Westwood. The bridge actually transversed the mill pond.

The main administrator for Red River in Westwood at this time was Fletcher Walker, one of T.B. Walker's sons. Fletcher Walker's house was a large lavish mansion erected at the far end of Westwood. The Red River Lumber Company soon set about constructing the buildings and structures that constituted the town of Westwood itself.

The town houses were all built on a planned sequence in rows. Streets were laid out, all either parallel or perpendicular to each other. The houses were all of wood construction (naturally) and were not painted outside nor inside. Eventually about 650 houses were built in Westwood . The rent for a family house was about $10 to $21 per month, depending on the size. For single transient workers two large bunkhouses, called clubhouses, were constructed. The clubhouse was sub-divided into small two-man rooms, and steam heated from a central boiler house. Each room had hot water but the men had to go to the barber shop to bathe. The cost at the barbershop was 25 cents for soap, water and a towel.

The Westwood family houses, however, had wood burning stoves or heaters for warmth, as well as inside toilets and water. (This plumbing arrangement however, did not apply to the homes in Old Town). Electricity was also provided and the inhabitants were charged 25 cents/ month per lightbulb. The Company provided daily garbage pick-up service as well as snow removal plows in the winter to keep the dirt streets reasonably clear.

Westwood was truly a Company town. There was no private ownership of real property, nor were there any deeds for property. Red River was the sole owner of all housing and structures in the town; also they operated all the businesses, but local townspeople were hired to help run them. The housing was available only to employees of Red River. The Company ran a tight ship and if any resident "got out of line" they were summarily fired from their job and evicted from their Company house. For some reason alcoholism was a big problem in Westwood and surrounding areas. The town had a deputy sheriff and a justice of peace - but they were responsible to the Company and not the County.

Nevertheless, the Walkers tried to do good by their workers. A 20 bed hospital was constructed and was very well equipped for those times. The first doctor was Dr. Fred Davis who started to practice medicine in Westwood in 1913. Each worker was charged $1.00/month for hospital care as a form of prepaid medical insurance plan. The worker and his family received complete medical care for this amount at no additional cost.

Westwood had a Company department store that was a feature of the town; very likely it was one of the largest such stores ever built at the time. Originally it was 96 by 140 feet, but later a 96 by 105 feet extension was added. The store was festooned with hundreds of illuminated lights. It carried a large inventory and a stock of items of every imaginable kind; from food to other staples such as clothing that the Company thought its employees might need. Obviously the Company expected many worker dollars to be channeled back to its coffers via the store profits. The local residents had little choice but to buy there, since Westwood was an isolated community and there was no competition. Presumably, the Company did not "gouge" its employees; nevertheless, some people bought (furtively) from door-to-door peddlers, and via Sears and Montgomery Ward mail order houses.

Also, easy automatic credit against future earnings was provided; with monthly payment of bills owed just deducted from the worker's paychecks. So in all, these practices in fact made the workers more beholden to the Company. A peculiar feature of the store was that the customers had no direct access to many of the items in the store. They stood in the aisles while clerks obtained desired items off the shelves and assembled or packaged the goods for the patrons. This practice was especially prevalent in the grocery store. Nevertheless, as a forerunner to today's shopping malls, the Company store was a huge attraction to the people in the town. It served as a gathering place where people could meet and socialize with their other townfolk.

Early on, the town also constructed numerous other buildings. These included an opera house (later used as a movie theatre, since no opera companies wanted to come to Westwood), bakery, firehouse, poolhall, bowling alley, church, school, jailhouse, municipal service building, and Company headquarters building. The town also had a band and a baseball team. By 1914, about 1,400 men were on the payroll as business was good. Horse drawn carts and wagons were the order of the day, but a few motor vehicles were starting to be seen on the unpaved streets. For the large horse fleet, of course, large areas and barns had to be set aside to accommodate the animals.

By 1915, Mill B had burned down but Mill A was in full production. A box factory, housed in an enormous building (160 by 512 feet), was in full production in addition to the main lumber mill. Lumbering in those days was quite hazardous, and fatalities and severe injuries occurred quite often; especially at the mill. The operations were a large one and safety measures were not the best. The machinery was complex and the rush to push production schedules exposed many workers to hazards on-the-job. The handling of the large logs and congestion on the mill floors especially created many dangerous conditions.

WESTWOOD GROWS

During the World War 1 years, 1915-1918,

Westwood prospered, since lumber was a precious commodity for the war effort. Expansion continued at the mill with many unique and advanced machinery and methods improvements taking place. According to the "Westwood Independent" newspaper (soon called "The Westwood Sugar Pine") a peak employment of 1,700 workers was reached during 1917-1918. By 1918, Red River was shipping lumber not only to Southern California and Eastern U.S. markets, but overseas as well to the Far East, Africa, and Europe, for example. The tariff schedules and efficient operations of the mill, plus S.P. railroad rates and access over the hill to the east, provided good competitive advantages for Red River during these times.

The workforce grew to 2,200, but constantly had to be replaced at a high rate because men got restless and left. About 800 men per month were needed for replacement during 1919, for example. Recruitment of new workers was mostly from the Sacramento and San Francisco areas of California, and from Nevada, but also from as far away as Texas. During the early 1920's, the lumber business was cyclical, what with changing tariffs on lumber products, and competition. Also, because of poor cutting practices, the forests around Westwood were being decimated and the raw materials (trees) had to be obtained from further away. This factor started to increase the costs considerably. Nevertheless, the demand was still great for lumber products and as time progressed into the late 1920's, the town of Westwood was prospering and still growing.

About this time, two noteworthy events were recorded: In 1927, the pride of Westwood, a public high school was constructed and completed. Red River production facilities furnished most of the materials, including desks and cabinets, and Red River craftsmen designed and erected the school. Also, by this time, women were employed extensively in the mill itself, especially in the veneer plant. So all in all, times were good for this tiny community in Northern California.

BAD TIMES

But then, THE STOCK MARKET CRASH OF 1929 OCCURRED, FOLLOWED BY THE GREAT DEPRESSION! Westwood, like other communities in America, was hit hard. The town struggled mightily to stay afloat. The lumber products were of good quality, but the demand was down because people could not pay for the goods. Creditors abounded, and money was slow to come in to Red River. The 1930 census showed 4,602 residents in Westwood. By the end of 1930, wages had been reduced, along with prices for Company services, including room and house rent. Many people were laid off of work; Westwood had a town full of people with no place else to go. The Walkers tried to keep the mill going on a greatly reduced basis. However, T.B. Walker, the founder, had died in 1928 and the central figure that had held the lumber empire together was gone during those trying days. Inheritance taxes took their toll and the heirs were forced to borrow money to pay the U.S. government. They were strapped for cash. Red River had also issued bonds as a security to raise cash, but this was like a mortgage against the Company.

By this time the Walker family was land rich only. Their wealth was tied up in lumber and trees and land, but creditors wanted cash during those times in the early 1930's. In fact the bankers were threatening to shut the Company down and take over the properties. It turned out that one of the sons, Theodore, came up with a plan that helped at the time. His plan was to sell at a discount, the huge inventory of goods (not lumber) that the Company owned. The Walkers raised $500,000 in this fashion; and they were able to get the creditors off of their backs.

BETTER TIMES

By the mid-1930s, the lumber market and the economy in general, were brighter and things looked better for the town of Westwood. About this time however, another problem had reared its ugly head. A large factory operation like that at Westwood maintained its competitive advantage because of the huge volumes of lumber products that it produced. However, the large lumber mills devoured the forest around it rapidly; and the logs had to be hauled longer and longer distances in order to get to the mill. This longer log movement, in turn, offset some of the cost advantage of mass production. In principle, for every lumber mill, there is some distance beyond which it cannot haul logs and still compete in the market place. The Company tried to set up small mills in the forest areas and this worked to a small extent. However this was not a good overall solution. Red River in fact was now paying for earlier poor forestry practices and the wanton clear cutting of trees during the many years of its operations.

Nevertheless, plant expansion continued in Westwood during the 1930's, and when World War 2 came in 1941, once again lumber products were in brisk demand. During this period Theodore Walker was called to active duty and his brother Willis died in 1942. By this time, of the 6 sons and 2 daughters and wife of T. B. Walker, only 2 sons survived. The plants reached maximum capacity in 1942; but by 1943 there weren't enough men left to run the mill because of the draft and war effort. This was ironic because lumber was now much in demand as a strategic country resource.

WESTWOOD OPERATIONS END

Abruptly in 1944, Red River Lumber Company decided to end its corporate existence and go out of the lumber business! The decision was a painful one. But it had been 15 years since T.B. Walker had died, and many of the heirs and grandchildren did not want to run the family business; they wanted to liquidate the family holdings, get their inheritance, and go about doing other things. Fruit Growers Supply Company, which had operated a good size lumber mill of its own in Susanville for many years, became the purchaser of the Red River Lumber Company in 1945. This Company operated the Westwood facility until about 1956. The 1950 census showed 3,618 residents in Westwood, but by 1956 only about 200 men were on the payroll. Fruit Growers decided to give up the Westwood operations in 1956 and all items and facilities went on sale. Mysteriously, the mill burned to the ground on November 8, 1956. Westwood, as a vibrant lumber town, in effect vanished on this date!

NOTE: This historical summary was put together by Jess R. Herrera using information obtained from a book by Robert M. Hanft, titled "Red River"; Published by the Center For Business and Economic Research, California State University, Chico, CA. 95929; 1st Printing: September, 1980, 2nd Printing, October, 1981. Library of Congress Cat. Card No. 79-53190, ISBN 0-9602894-5-3. The book is no longer in print but a copy was borrowed from Bill Hadley, a friend from P.G.&E. Company.

Index